SAY IT . . . RIGHT

ALSO BY LILLIAN GLASS, PH.D.

Talk to Win
How to Deprogram Your Valley Girl

SAY IT . . . RIGHT

How to Talk in Any
Social or Business Situation

LILLIAN GLASS, Ph.D.

A PERIGEE BOOK

TO LAMBEAR—
*who's taught me what unconditional love and
real communication are all about.*

Perigee Books
are published by
The Berkley Publishing Group
200 Madison Avenue
New York, New York 10016

First Perigee Edition 1992

Library of Congress Cataloging-in-Publication Data

Glass, Lillian.
Say it...right : how to talk in any social or business situation /
Lillian Glass. — First Perigee ed.
p.   cm.
Includes index.
ISBN 0-399-51699-9 (acid-free paper)
1. Oral communication.   2. Etiquette.   I. Title.
[P95.G53   1992]   91-14370   CIP
808.56—dc20

Cover design © 1991 by Dorothy Wachtenheim
Front cover photograph © by Harry Langdon
Hair and makeup by Jeff Jones

Printed in the United States of America
9   10   11   12   13   14   15

This book is printed on acid-free paper.
∞

ACKNOWLEDGMENTS

You are only as great as the shoulders you stand on and I've been blessed to have stood on some pretty great shoulders. I wish to acknowledge my heroes for whom I have ultimate respect and admiration—people who have enriched my life and who have made an impact on how I communicate.

Susan Grode—my agent, attorney, friend, and role model. Adrienne Ingrum, my wonderful editor and supportive friend, Rosalie Glass, my mother and friend. Christopher Lambert, George Nelson Case, Sean Connery, Marlee Matlin, Reverend Jesse Jackson, Julio Iglesias, Lili Zanuck, Dustin Hoffman, Donald Trump, Barbara Walters, Norman Brokaw, Harry Langdon, Jeff Jones, Merv Griffin, Jerry Bruckheimer, Ben Vereen, Doctor Edward A. Kantor, Doctor Joseph Sugarman, Greg Gorman, Mickey Rourke, Al Davis, Mayor Tom Bradley, Doctor Henry Kawamoto, Mr. Blackwell, Burt Lancaster, Doctor Robert J. Gorlin, Colleen Camp, Dolph Lundgren, Donna Hennen, Doctor H. Harlan Bloomer, Paul Bloch, Kirk Douglas, Bikrum Choudhury, Senator Albert Gore, Arnold Kopelson, Nicky Blair, Rita Coolidge, Lew Wasserman, Carol Isenberg, Doctor Bernard Geltzer, Judge Judith Stein, Mona Thalheimer, Doctor Perry Crenshaw, Doctor Henry Yamada, June Gabora, Dale Neff, Doctor Maxine Ostrum, Lynn Della Guardia, Pam Kemp, Lee Iacocca, Traci Hunt, Rick Cramer, Jeff Kramer, Rene Russo, Sue Kiel, Barbara K. Ratliff, Bob Rafelson, Ana Alicia, Bob Cummings, Melanie Griffith, President George Bush, John LeMaire, Kathleen Turner, Sheri Sylvester, Sylvester Stallone, Charlie Minor, Bill Farley, Kirk Kilgour, Seth Riggs, Shirley Temple Black, Bill Cosby, Vidal Sassoon, Rod Martin, Jerry Dunphy, Chuck Norris, David Gamburg, Dolly Parton, Michael Eisner, Bette Midler, Francine Drescher, Terry McQueen, Georgia Frontiere, John Forsythe, Cecilia and

Diana Bolocco, Michael Young, Sally and Ivor Davis, Bill Sharman, Doctor Norman Martin, Shadoe Stevens, Jake Steinfeld, Bob and June Easton, Doctor William Perkins, Roseanne Barr, Doctor Daniel Boone, Beth Roll, Alan Miller, Rob Lowe, Gloria Loring, Sinbad, Olivia Newton-John, Matt Lattanzi, Sela Ward, Wanna McMahon, Jackie-Joyner Kersee, Florence Griffith Joyner, Lester Hayes, Edward James Olmos, Costas Mendalore, Sally Kirkland, Richard Fore, Harvey Sarles, Billy Crystal, Donna Dixon, Dan Akroyd, Jim Eason, Doctor James H. Mullendore, Rob Reiner, Robert Cassidy, George Armstrong, Frances Hernandez, Susan Shane, Marcy Carsey.

Contents

Talking to Subordinates
Talking to Police Officers
Vocal Self-Defense

Introduction

Have you ever not known what to say in a particular situation?

Have you ever wanted to say something but felt too self-conscious?

Have you ever been invited to an important dinner or a party and wondered: What will I say? What if I sound stupid? What if there's a lull in the conversation—do I just sit there or keep talking?

Well, you're not alone. As a communications specialist, I have seen even the boldest businessmen turn pale at the thought of attending a black-tie affair, speaking at a board meeting, or just meeting new people. I have watched people cry at the mere thought of a new social interaction.

According to *The Book of Lists,* the number-one fear in society today is the fear of talking in front of other people.

It's not so surprising. After all, in school we are taught many new things, but nobody teaches us how to communicate with one another.

I have been fortunate enough to work with thousands of people, from the most severely handicapped to the hottest stars in Hollywood—stars like Dustin Hoffman, whom I helped prepare for his role in *Tootsie,* and Julio Iglesias. I helped Swedish actor Dolph Lundgren and the French actor Christopher Lambert speak with American accents. I was able to help Ben Vereen become a sought-after television host, and my work with the wonderfully talented Marlee Matlin helped make her speaking debut as an Academy–Award presenter before millions of viewers.

Everybody has the power to become a terrific communicator—not just stars. It's a matter of confronting your fears in different situations and learning to feel good about yourself.

Communication is not just verbal. Good communication is visual, sensual, and aural. It's not being afraid to be enthusiastic and spontaneous. It's not being afraid to express yourself or reach out to others.

I learned early on that I could *make* things happen, instead of sitting back and waiting for things to happen or for others to do things for me. Positive things happened when I took the risk of communicating my needs and wants. By openly expressing myself and using all of my senses, I was able to improve the quality of my own life and the lives of the thousands of my clients. I've taught them communication strategies that work. In this book I am sharing these same techniques with you.

There is perhaps nothing more frustrating than not being able to communicate. I first became aware of this when I was ten years old and watched an Easter Seals telethon on TV. Many children, some who were even my age at the time, were unable to talk. They couldn't even say, "Hi, how are you?" or what they wanted for lunch. Saliva drooled from their mouths. I cried for these children. But when I watched a speech therapist teach a ten-year-old girl with cerebral palsy to speak, my tears stopped. The therapist was able to help the girl to make a string of sounds and eventually speak a meaningful sentence. It was then that I decided what I would be when I grew up. I thought that my life would be fulfilled if I could be a catalyst like that speech therapist and help others experience the joy I felt in talking with people.

I took my education to the highest level possible, and while I have accumulated many honors along the way, my best rewards have been personal ones. I was able to break new ground in speech pathology by examining the effects of speech on various genetic diseases where voice and speech patterns could be helpful in diagnosing certain genetic diseases.

As a researcher and professor I worked with people who had such genetic abnormalities as dwarfism, neurofibromatosis (the Elephant Man disease), and people like Rocky Dennis, the boy in the movie *Mask*. I found that if they communicated better, others were more likely to overlook their physical disfigurements.

I also learned that no how matter how different a person is, they really are more like us than we realize. Every human being experiences the same feelings, the same hurts. We all suffer from the same loneliness and have the same need to express our needs and feelings to other people. Deep down inside we all need love and attention. We all hunger for love, for self-respect, and acceptance. We all hunger to be creative and have a meaningful place in this world. With world events taking a more positive turn, with countries uniting and walls tumbling down, walls between people also need to come down in order for more effective human relations to occur.

Throughout my professional life I've been able to witness my share of little miracles. A deaf boy who had never spoken before became a client, and now, after one year, people can understand him.

Lester Hayes, the five-time all-pro cornerback for the Los Angeles Raiders, was a severe stutterer. After catching a winning pass at the Superbowl, the press descended on him with cameras and microphones. His face contorted as he uncontrollably twitched his eyes and stuck out his tongue but no words came out. Then millions of viewers on national TV heard a series of motor-like purrs, repeated sounds, and catatonic pauses that seemed to last forever. Yet Lester's worst nightmare became an opportunity for dramatic growth. Soon after we committed to working together, he was able to talk through press conferences without stuttering, and now he delivers motivational speeches to hundreds of students and businessmen.

Sean Connery, one of the world's greatest actors, for years hurt his vocal cords through improper speech habits. His voice cracked and even became weakened due to improper breath support. (You can even hear it in his early James Bond movies.) Today he's got a richer, smoother, more resonant tone. He called me from the set of his last film to tell me that the work we did together literally saved his voice.

I love working with stars—not just movie stars, but people who are stars in their fields. You can be a star, too, by knowing how to communicate well in any situation. This book will teach you how. It came about because of the thousands of letters I received from people in response to the second half of my book *Talk to Win* (Putnam, 1987), which focused on self-esteem and developing good communication skills. Many readers told me they were inspired to develop better communication skills by the examples I shared in the book.

When clients come to me to work on their voice and speech skills, they discover that they also learn to talk more effectively to everyone.

Inspired by case histories from my own experiences with clients and friends, I have come up with formulas that can help you solve your communication problems. In this book you will learn exactly what to say to anyone in almost any situation. You will meet people who are like you and feel just like you do. You'll see what they did to improve the way they relate to others. In doing so, you will grow with them.

This book can improve the quality of your life, as well as the quality of the lives of those around you. It will help you talk to people you don't know, and talk more effectively with people you do know. It will help you find the right words for the right occasion. It will show you how to diffuse inappropriate anger and how to express legitimate anger and how to tell the difference between the two. It will help you communicate better in your personal and professional relationships. It can even help you make more money. In essence, this book will increase your self-confidence! When you become a better communicator, it's amazing how your whole life changes for the better. I've seen it time and time again.

After reading this book, you'll never feel at a loss for words again!

DR. LILLIAN GLASS

... 1 ...

"Pleased to Meet You"

Jennifer looked across the room and her heart literally skipped a beat as she saw the man of her dreams. He was tall, handsome, and knew how to dress. Anxious to meet him, she immediately got her friend Becky, the hostess, to introduce her to him.

"Mark," Becky said enthusiastically, "I want you to meet a great friend of mine, Jennifer. Jennifer, this is Mark." Mark did not stand up but merely glanced at the two women and said, "Oh, hi," and then averted his eyes and looked down.

After a few uncomfortable moments, Jennifer excused herself to get something to drink. She never looked back, and never gave him another thought.

Six months later, Jennifer found herself seated next to Mark at a black-tie affair hosted by another mutual friend. Jennifer was disappointed when she saw that her dinner partner was Mark, and thought to herself, "This is going to be a *long* evening."

To her surprise, Mark was anything but indifferent to her at their second meeting. He seemed excited to see her, and told her that he couldn't understand why she left so abruptly when they were introduced at Becky's party.

She then told him that she thought he didn't want anything

to do with her. She told him how he didn't even get up to shake her hand or even look at her. Mark then replied that he had actually been very attracted to her—so much so, he said, that it made him feel shy and uncomfortable. However, when he finally did get his nerve up to talk to her, she had already left.

Jennifer and Mark spent the rest of the evening talking and finding out that they had much in common. Once he relaxed, she found Mark to be personable, warm, and to have a great sense of humor. At the end of the evening, she told him she was glad that she had another opportunity to meet him. Mark told her that he was used to her comment since most people, he said, have a negative first impression of him because his shyness and self-consciousness always initially seemed to get in the way.

Mark and Jennifer were fortunate that they had a second chance, but many people aren't that lucky.

Research has shown that you can tell in the first four minutes of meeting someone whether a person is going to be your friend, your lover, or simply an acquaintance. You can see, by Jennifer and Mark's first meeting, how important first impressions are, and how giving off the wrong cues can sabotage you socially. The same holds true for the business world.

One of my clients, Jack, a businessman, who took over his father's office supply company when his father retired, was having a difficult time meeting new clients. Unlike his father, who was very outgoing and gregarious, Jack was very shy and withdrawn. His handshake and his voice were both weak. Every time he met a new client, he would break into a cold sweat and couldn't even look that person in the eye.

His awkwardness made his customers feel so uncomfortable that it cost him a lot of business, which strained the relations between Jack and his father.

By teaching Jack a simple breathing exercise to release tension, how to smile and look people in the eye when he met them, how to have a firmer handshake, and how to stop thinking about how he was coming across and start concentrating on *what* he was trying to say instead, he became more likeable. By becoming more interested in his clients and by not trying to be as entertaining and witty as his father, or comparing himself to his father, he made a complete turnaround both personally and professionally. As well, his business has doubled. He has become more self-confident, and his father has more respect for Jack as the new head of the family business.

Both Jennifer's and Jack's experiences show us how important a simple greeting can be.

FOUR STEPS TOWARD BEING A BETTER GREETER

1. SMILE

The first thing you need to do to greet another person is forget about your own problems or concerns and smile. No matter what it takes, smile. Research shows it takes less muscles to smile than frown, so by smiling, you are even helping to release your tensions. When you greet someone, your smile is the most effective way of showing someone that you are interested in them and what they have to say because a smile conveys warmth and openness. If you don't like the way you smile, look in the mirror or videotape yourself so you can improve the way you smile. Oftentimes, people don't like the way they smile because they don't like the way their teeth look. If you don't like the way your teeth look when you smile, see a dentist. I have sent countless people who were self-conscious about their smile because of the condition of their teeth to Dr. Henry Yamada and have seen miracles happen as they gained more confidence and were no longer afraid to show off their teeth when they smiled. In some cases, old habits die hard, so I retrain people to use their facial muscles to smile by having them look into the mirror or videotaping them.

So don't let your teeth stop you from smiling. Remember, it's easier to fix your teeth and your smile than all the bad impressions created by not smiling.

2. FACIAL CONTACT

Most people have no idea what a negative, alienating effect poor eye contact can have on their "total image." Looking up or down or from side to side when you are meeting someone gives the impression that you are shifty and cannot be trusted, or that you're not interested in them or bored.

This doesn't mean you should *stare* into a person's eyes, unless, of course, you are in love with that person. Staring usually can be threatening and disconcerting, and can make you feel uncomfortable or even threatened.

You need to make *facial contact*, not just eye contact, by looking at the person's "total face." Look at their forehead, hair, nose, and their chin as well as their eyes. Here is a simple exercise to help you make better facial contact with people.

The next time you're having a conversation with someone, look at their whole face for five seconds. *Next*, look at each part of the face for three seconds. *Then* look at the whole face for six seconds, the eyes for three seconds, and at each part of the face for three seconds.

Then, alternate between focusing on the whole face for three seconds and each part of the face at three-second intervals.

If you practice this technique when you first meet someone, you will be surprised at how comfortable you will both feel.

3. SHAKING HANDS

I once had a client who was six foot five with a very wimpy handshake. He was not a wimpy person but was simply afraid of intimidating people because of his extraordinary size. Therefore, he shook hands in such a seemingly non-threatening way that his presence was diminished. People who shook hands with him were instantly disappointed because his initial impression of size and power was so incongruous with his weak handshake. When he finally improved his handshake, he noticed that people treated him differently. He felt that they seemed to respect him more now. Whether we want to admit it or not, we tend to make judgments of others by the way they shake our hands. For example, the looser the handshake is, the less confidence is communicated. Too tight a grip may be interpreted as inner aggression, or a desire to dominate the relationship, so be aware of that. You want to have a firm handshake, held for about three seconds. This indicates confidence and self-assuredness.

If you want to convey warmth and show that you really like the other person, you need to greet them with the double hand-shake. Put your left hand on top of the other person's right hand while you shake hands. The next time you meet someone you really like, try cupping his or her hand in both of yours as this often conveys a great deal of warmth in your communication.

If you plan to meet new people, you need to keep your hands ready for the handshake. If you are a woman who gets sweaty or clammy hands, keep a powder puff in your purse; men can keep a powder puff or handkerchief in a pocket. Wiping your hands on a dry puff or a handkerchief in your pocket can make a big difference in the impression you give through your hand-shake.

A warm, sincere handshake will definitely help you connect with another person. A woman client once said to me, "You know, I really liked you immediately because I felt you were so warm. You took my hand in yours without even thinking about it and shook it so firmly." That handshake was even more sig-nificant since this woman did not have normally shaped hands. She had a birth defect—"Lobster Claw" hands—a genetic dis-order where the fingers are fused together in a mitt-like fashion. She was so surprised when I reached out and grabbed her hand and held it and shook it just like I would anyone else's, because she wasn't used to people feeling comfortable with her hands. So remember, an effective handshake can create immediate openness.

4. WARM "HELLO"

When you greet people, don't be afraid to show enthusiasm: "I'm really thrilled to meet you," or "I've heard so many won-derful things about you." Such greetings open things up posi-tively.

It is *not* a good idea to start off with "How are you?" when you greet a stranger. So often this is a meaningless, overused, throw-away expression. Most of the time, the person who is using it has no real desire to know how the other person actually is. It can also be very intrusive. Most people just end up lying and say, "Fine. How are you?" when they neither feel fine nor care how you are. If you don't really want to know how a person is, *DON'T ASK.* Otherwise it may sound phoney. Never try to fake emotions. It breeds insincerity and in a subtle way does not do much for your self-esteem.

We all need to stop communicating with words that *mean nothing*. Your words are your tools, and every tool has to be used with a specific *intention* in mind. So know the reason why you are saying what you say.

A greeting should be positive. Look right at the person, smile, say "Nice to meet you," and with a smile and a firm handshake you are off to a good start in getting to know someone new or getting to know someone even better.

If you really want to know how someone is, ask them sincerely. If you could hear me say "How are you?" it would sound like this: "How *ARE YOU?*" Punch up the words "are" and "you" by using a louder tone and a more upward inflection.

It's important to always express your real feelings by using the right emotional tones.

A warm smile, good facial contact, a firm handshake, and a warm hello are the building blocks to being a successful greeter.

TO KISS OR NOT TO KISS

Have you ever wondered when, where, how, and *if* it was right to kiss someone when you greet them? Well, you're not alone.

Kissing can also be a very cultural thing. I was once a judge at the Miss USA Pageant. A former Miss Universe, Cecilia Bolocco of Chile, was a judge with me. She brought her ten-year-old sister, Diana, along with her. When this little girl met me and the other judges, she kissed us on both cheeks. When she left us, she kissed us again on both cheeks, which is a Latin American custom. Her gesture warmed the hearts of all the judges, and endeared her to all of us.

In Latin American countries and in Europe, kissing is quite common—men kissing men, women kissing women, as well as women kissing men and men kissing women. In the United States, unfortunately, people seem to be more uptight about customary kissing, though in some places, like Hollywood, California, it's common to kiss on the cheek or lips when you greet someone you know. Kissing often helps to break the ice and bring you closer to that person faster.

If you feel compatible and warm with a person, there is no reason why you can't greet them with a kiss. Recently, the newspaper *USA Today* reported that basketball superstars Magic Johnson and Isiah Thomas greet each other with kisses on the court. An article ensued concerning whether it was proper for men to kiss men when they greet one another. I say, of course men can kiss men. Men all over Europe and Latin America have been doing it for centuries. Here in America, television host Arsenio Hall sometimes kisses his male guests, and the late Sammy Davis, Jr., and his other entertainer friends like Frank Sinatra, Dean Martin, and Jerry Lewis kissed each other in public for years. Kissing is a warm, loving, tender, HUMAN gesture and we ALL need to do it and not be ashamed of it.

I was once in a restaurant where I saw a father greet his son, whom it appeared he had not seen for a while, with a kiss on the lips. I was moved by this tender display of father-son affection. Men should feel more free to kiss each other. Women should feel more comfortable as well. Kissing a member of the same sex does not necessarily connote lesbian or gay behavior.

Unfortunately, many of us have been raised according to the Skinnerian approach of the 1940s and 1950s—not cuddling your children and letting them cry until they stop. How sad it was that we did not realize earlier how psychologically dangerous and inappropriate this behavior was. Lack of early affection can create an adult who has tremendous difficulty communicating with others in every way. We need to be more demonstrative in our affection toward other people.

Who and when you kiss is up to you. Like actors, who are trained to know their intention in everything they do when they perform, you, too, have to know your intentions when you are interacting with others. You have to ask yourself, *Do I really feel warm toward this person?* A kiss can be one of the most powerful gestures you can do, so when you do kiss someone, be sure that it is a kiss where skin touches skin—not air. I have seen all too many socialites "kiss air" when they don't want to mess up each other's makeup. "Hi, dahling," they say to one another, and then they kiss the air without even touching cheeks. To the person watching this, it looks insincere, and to the person receiving this kiss it feels even more insincere. Don't be afraid to mess up your makeup. You can repair it in the bathroom afterwards—or if you are that worried—then give the person a big hug.

TO HUG OR NOT TO HUG

The same principles that govern kissing govern hugging. You certainly need to feel free to touch another person, but at the same time you want to have respect for the other person's physical space. Most of us vary in our need for physical contact. For some, even the slightest, most casual contact can make them extremely uncomfortable. A few years ago many seminars and workbooks advocated "free hugging," so many people were into openly hugging practically everyone they met. Hugging is fine when it is situationally appropriate, but it can become quite intrusive or invasive when it is not appropriate.

It is in your best interest to hug only when it is situationally appropriate—when you *really* like the other person and you want to embrace them. Once again, there's nothing wrong with men hugging men and women hugging women in public. It can be endearing and oftentimes can bring people even closer together.

STOPPING THE I THINK THAT YOU THINK THAT I THINK GAME

Why is it that people are so afraid to meet new people? Have world affairs really made us all that afraid of each other or xenophobic?

Actually, a lot of our fears come from a little game we play with ourselves called *I think that you think that I think*. We are so busy thinking about what we think the other person thinks of us that we lose sight of what we actually want to say to them. In essence, we are so busy thinking about whether *we are making a good impression* that we become nervous and self-conscious. We stop being ourselves.

I recently met Mr. Blackwell—the world's leading clothing critic. Every year Mr. Blackwell puts out his eagerly awaited and equally dreaded list of the "10 Best" and "10 Worst" dressers. I was initially nervous about meeting the great Mr. Blackwell. While I was getting ready to leave for the dinner party, I started thinking, "I hope I'm dressed well enough . . . I hope he thinks I look okay . . . I wonder what he'll find wrong with my dress." Wearing my most elegant Chanel outfit, I figured that if he was going to judge me, he was going to have to criticize designer Karl Lagerfeld.

At the dinner party, we were finally introduced—"Mr. Blackwell, this is Dr. Lillian Glass. Dr. Glass, this is Mr. Blackwell"—as we were seated next to one another.

I could feel myself getting nervous and experiencing shortness of breath. I wanted to make a good impression. I didn't want him to write bad things about me or my outfit in his column.

Then I thought to myself, "This is ridiculous. Change your attitude. Stop being so self-conscious because it's standing in the way of *you* being *you*. You're here just to have a good time, so just enjoy yourself." And I did just that and ended up having a great time. Mr. Blackwell and I talked the entire evening and he turned out to be a fabulous person—witty, charming, and nonjudgmental. He was completely different from the person I had imagined from reading his columns and seeing him on television.

I was equally surprised to find out through the course of our conversation that he had been just as nervous about meeting me as I was about meeting him. He had heard positive things about me from mutual friends, had read my previous book, *Talk to Win*, and had also seen me on television. "I was hoping that you would think my speech was okay," he told me, as we both laughed.

We were both playing the *I think that you think that I think* game. Almost all of us play this little mind game with ourselves at one time or another. Doing this can hinder your ability to meet people. By playing this game with yourself, you lose sight of what you have to say—or what the other person really has to offer. Had Mr. Blackwell and I held onto our preconceptions and continued to play the *I think that you think that I think* game with ourselves, we wouldn't have had a very good time with one another. Because we both consciously stopped playing the game and let down our defenses and ignored our insecurities, we felt completely comfortable with one another and became friends by the end of the evening.

The best way to stop the *I think that you think that I think* record from playing itself over and over in your head is to concentrate on becoming more *interested* than *interesting*. Just say to yourself, "I am playing the *I think that you think that I think* game again and I'm not having fun," and then proceed to draw the other person out by asking them questions about themselves or about current topics of interest.

Instead of indulging in your fear of meeting new people, look at these encounters as exciting challenges and adventures. Once you stop playing the *I think that you think that I think* game and become more interested than interesting you will never again feel insecure about meeting anyone.

HELP FOR THE BREATHLESS

Actor Christopher Lambert of *Greystoke: The Legend of Tarzan* and *Highlander* I and II is sexy and handsome. There's no doubt about that. He's also got charisma and presence. One day, after one of our sessions, Christopher happened to walk by another of my clients, Annette, a young female attorney who was seated in my waiting room. When she entered my office for her appointment, she was all flushed and her neck was starting to break out in red blotches. She was short of breath and seemed to be in a state of shock. "Was that Christopher Lambert who just left?" she asked. When I told her yes, it was, she let out a scream.

"Oh, my God, I love Christopher Lambert. I can't believe I just saw Christopher Lambert and he said 'Hi' to me. I can't believe it! I'll never be the same."

All of a sudden, this mature young attorney had regressed to a star-struck teenager swooning over her screen idol!

I am used to seeing celebrities—some of the biggest stars and politicians have come into my office—yet my heart has pounded a bit harder as well for people I've admired. It happens to all of us. You may have come close to it yourself. Your heart may have started to beat fast, your breath may have become short, or you may have even started to hyperventilate or get dizzy when you've met someone you've always admired.

At times like this, there is nothing you can do about the adrenaline rushing through your body. However, there is something you can do to regain your composure immediately. Take a deep breath in through your mouth, hold it for three seconds, and then slowly let it out. *Holding in* the breath is the important thing—for three whole seconds (just count one potato, two potato, three potato)—and then slowly blow the air out through your mouth. In no time you will regain control of yourself. If you do this subtly, nobody will notice the technique you are using to get your "heart put back in its proper place."

Do this exercise two or three times if necessary while you are continuing to look at that person. Just keep taking a breath in, hold it, and then slowly release the air. Do this until you have oxygenated yourself, until you have regained your equilibrium and no longer feel light-headed.

The next thing you want to do is establish good posture. Having a good sense of body posture can enhance your confidence as you approach people. Tighten up your buttocks and hold your head up by pretending there's a string holding it up at the crown. Roll one shoulder back and keep it there and then roll the other shoulder back. Doing this will help you to feel more confident and in control. Now you are ready to meet that person you've always wanted to meet. Walk directly over to them and smile while you say "Hello."

MEETING PUBLIC FIGURES

People in public life are just like you. They have the same feelings and sensitivities you do. Most public figures realize that it is their fans—the public—who have put them where they are, so most of them will be responsive to you, providing that you treat them with warmth and respect. This means not disturbing them when they are eating or heavily engaged in conversation. If you want to meet someone you've always admired, whether they are famous or not, all you have to do is get your confidence level up by using the breathing and the posture techniques.

One Christmas, I was at a party in Aspen, Colorado, and Donald Trump was there. I had always been a big fan of Donald Trump because he is a *doer* who makes things happen. I wanted to meet him. My friend Bill Farley, chairman of Farley Industries and CEO of Fruit of the Loom, asked if I would like to meet him. As I walked across the room toward Mr. Trump, I kept doing the breathing exercise I described earlier. While doing this exercise, many thoughts ran through my head—*What will I say to him? What will we talk about?* I took my breath in, held it, rolled my shoulders back, and stood straight, which enabled me to gain composure and confidence. Bill Farley, I might add, was also an excellent introducer, which, of course, helped. "Donald Trump," he said, "this is Dr. Lillian Glass, a world-renowned speech and communication specialist. You both have something in common as she also wrote a top-selling book, *Talk to Win.*" Mr. Trump and I then chatted a while and ended up sending one another our respective books.

BRING ALONG YOUR FAN

My meeting Mr. Trump illustrates how helpful it can be to have someone introduce you who knows exactly how to make you appear in the best light. The best way to meet people is to be introduced to them by someone else. It makes you seem more credible and more important when you have a spokesperson singing your praises. When you go to a party where your intention is to meet new people, it's an excellent idea to bring along a "fan"— a person who supports, respects, and admires you and whom you feel the same about. Bringing my friend Bill Farley to the party in Aspen allowed me to promote him to my celebrity friends, while he promoted me to his political and business friends.

Your fan can be your best friend, a spouse, or anyone who respects you and who will promote you to the other guests in a way that will impress others while they are introducing you, because most of us tend to be bolder when we introduce a friend than when we introduce ourselves.

A friend of mine, Lisa, wanted to meet a rock star that we both saw at a party one evening. Neither Lisa nor I knew the star, but she was absolutely dying to meet him. So I went right up to him with Lisa when he was standing alone and said, "Hi, I'm Lillian Glass and this is my friend Lisa Jones who has every album you ever made." The rock singer was flattered and after talking to Lisa all evening ended up dating her.

So the next time you go to a party, bring a "fan" along who's really on your side. You can even encourage them to introduce you to anyone you want to meet and reciprocate by doing the same for them.

BEING A PROMOTER

When you introduce two people to one another, you need to know something about them before you introduce them—in order to find a common bond between them so that they can easily have something to talk about after you introduce them. It may be that they both like opera, or that they are both "outdoorsy." Or it may be that they both have Ph.D.s or that they both came from the same town.

When introducing people, you need to be honest and open and not hold back any of your good feelings about them so that you "promote" them to each other. Instead of saying, "Fred, I'd like you to meet a good friend of mine—Clarissa," give Fred some more information about Clarissa. Be generous in your praise of her and elaborate on who she is—even if the two of them seem to have nothing in common.

You may say, "Fred, I'd like you to meet a very dear friend of mine, Clarissa. Clarissa is a dancer but she's also a gourmet cook who's studied in France." By giving out more information, Clarissa appears to be a more interesting person to talk to. The introduction opens up numerous topics of discussion, such as dancing, food, France and schooling, how she and the host became friends. In essence, the more information you give about the other person the more chances they will have something in common—something of interest to talk about.

INTRODUCING YOURSELF

What do you do when you want to meet someone but nobody is around to introduce you to them? How do you let the other person know how great you are without coming across as pompous and obnoxious?

There is an art to introducing yourself. The first thing you need to do, of course, is smile, put out your hand, say hello in a confident manner, and give a summary statement of what you do. For example: "Hi, I'm Shiela Jason and I'm a tax attorney in Orange County." You don't want to just say "I'm an attorney." Tell the person what kind of attorney you are or what company you work for. The more information you give in the shortest period of time, the better your communication exchange will be. Doing this encourages the other person to respond to what you do. For example, "My brother is a tax attorney," or "I live in Orange County, too," so giving more information about yourself serves as *conversation bait*.

You may also mention something that you both have in common. An introduction such as, "Hi, I'm Shiela Jason and I saw you at the Jacksons' party two years ago," opens up an easy discussion about the Jacksons and other people you might both know.

While introducing yourself, you need to eliminate any negative thoughts or expectations of how that person is going to react to your words based on what you have heard about them. Just because you heard that they were arrogant and caustic with someone else doesn't mean it is true, or that they will be that way with you. So try to keep an open mind when you introduce yourself to others.

Remember never to go on and on about yourself. Be concise and present the key points about who you are in an up-beat, positive manner.

RE-INTRODUCING YOURSELF

Carla and Tony were at a party and they saw Tony's friend, Gary. Tony said, "Hi Carla, I want to introduce you to Gary."

"No way," Carla said. "I don't ever want to meet him again. I've been introduced to him five times and he never remembers who I am."

I can't begin to tell you how many clients have told me how they intensely disliked someone for forgetting them. I can't say that I blame them, because what these "forgetters" are actually saying to them is "You're not that important to me" or "You didn't impress me enough to remember you or even your name."

If someone forgets who you are, they may have a short memory, so don't be afraid to remind them where they met you and what the circumstances were, even though it may embarrass them when they finally do remember. Perhaps they don't remember you because you have changed physically since they met you—your hairstyle or your weight or the circumstances of your life. One of my clients, Gina, dyed her hair blond, got a nose job, had her eyes done, and got a chin implant, so she had no right to be offended when nobody recognized her. My advice to Gina was to start re-introducing herself to people she knew by going up to them at social gatherings, putting her hand out, and saying, "Hi, I'm Gina Grayson—how are you?" This eliminated any awkwardness or embarrassment on her part and on the part of those who didn't recognize her, and also got her a lot of compliments because everyone told her how terrific she looked.

Don't feel awkward about re-introducing yourself. Just smile, put out your hand, and reaffirm your name in their memory.

FORGETTING A PERSON'S NAME

What do you do if *you* forget a person's name? This is an embarrassing situation, but we have all faced it at one time or another. There are several options, depending on the situation. If you have just met, you can be apologetic and simply ask the person to repeat their name. Or you may ask, "How do you pronounce your name?" If, on the other hand, you feel that letting the other person know you have forgotten their name might greatly offend them, excuse yourself momentarily and find someone else at the party who knows their name and then return immediately.

An accountant friend of mind was in a very embarrassing situation at an office party. He was just about to introduce his wife to a new accountant in the firm when he realized that he had suddenly blanked on the person's name. What could he do? He decided to diffuse the awkward dilemma and his anxiety by making a joke of it. "I can't believe this," he said. "I must be losing brain cells—too much champagne! I've just drawn a complete blank on your name, and I wanted to introduce you to my wife." Then he turned to his wife and said, "What did you say *your* name was?"

The accountant held out his hand to my client's wife and said, "Hi, I'm Alex Gordon," and she replied, "I'm Sandy Goodman." She then turned to her husband and good-naturedly said, "Now you've got both of our names—so don't forget them again!" and all three laughed.

Both my client and his wife, of course, managed to diffuse an embarrassing situation by using humor. So be direct and open, and try to pull out your sense of humor if all else fails.

HOW TO REMEMBER A PERSON'S NAME

There are effective ways of improving your ability to remember names as well as the faces that go with them.

If you have difficulty remembering names when you meet new people, "branding" the name in your mind by associating the name you hear with a word or a visual symbol is essential to engrain the name in your memory. For example, if you are introduced to a person whose name is Frank, you may want to brand him in your mind as being very *frank*—very honest. If a person's name is Fred and he sounds boring, you might want to think of "Dead Fred" (but keep it to yourself).

You can do the same thing with people's last names. If you are introduced to someone whose name is Steinfield, you may think that the word *stein* means stone in German and *field* as you imagine them in a field of stones. When you are branding someone's name in your mind, use all of your senses. Get as much of a visual, auditory, and sensual impression of the name as you can.

If a person tells you their name and you don't hear it, ask them to repeat it, and then you repeat it. If it sounds like an unusual name, don't be afraid to spell it or ask, "What's the derivation of the name?" This is also a good way of opening up a conversation. If someone mispronounces your name, don't be afraid to correct them and even spell it for them. This is all part of the branding process.

If you catch yourself calling a person by the wrong name, apologize and call them by their correct name immediately. If they happen to catch it, apologize and say the right name, and then repeat it in the conversation later on. Making up lame excuses for forgetting a person's name doesn't work. People can usually see through it. Sincerity and admitting you forgot their name is always better.

If someone mispronounces your name or calls you by the wrong name, by all means correct them, but do it politely.

Be sure to speak up when you tell someone your name. A lot of people mumble their names, as if they are ashamed of them. How you say your name actually says a lot about you. If you mumble your name, it may convey to people that you don't feel good about yourself, that you don't have a lot of confidence. If you say your name too fast, it may tell people that you do not consider yourself to be very important. If you say your name too loudly, you may appear to be obnoxious or conceited. If you do any of these things, you may be giving the wrong impression, even though you don't intend to do so.

If you want people to remember your name, just speak up and let the person know who you are, with warmth and openness.

IMPROVING THE WAY YOU GREET OTHERS

A client of mine, Alexandra, can walk in to a supermarket wearing gym clothes and no makeup, and so many people— men and women—will be smiling at her. Alexandra has a bounce in her step, a smile on her face, and acknowledges people as she goes.

Alexandra is upbeat and happy. That doesn't mean bad things don't come her way in life, but she handles them and doesn't carry her negative feelings with her into situations where negative feelings aren't warranted. She has an inner glow, and any place she goes she is the absolute star. Everything about her— her posture, her expression, the way she moves—radiates warmth. Unfortunately, many of us are walking around dreading life and waiting for the next bad thing to happen.

How can you become as upbeat and glowing as Alexandra? First, realize that a "sour look" is nothing more than a bad habit. Second, bring people and events into your life that will nourish you and enable you to feel better about yourself and the people around you. Surrounding yourself with loving friends and people who really care about you allows you to create a positive environment and live life with a positive, upbeat glow. Eliminate non-supportive, negative, non-nurturing people from your life and practice getting into the habit of being happy and appreciative.

ADDRESSING PEOPLE

Whenever you address another person, make sure that you repeat their name. This not only brands their name into your memory, but it endears that person to you as they subconsciously "register" that you are interested in them. Today, married women often-times keep their maiden names and some men even hyphenate their wife's maiden name with their own last name. Always respect their wishes and use the name *they* want to use.

Never take the liberty of using a person's first name unless they invite you to do so. Address all people as *Mr.* or *Mrs.*, or *Ms.*, until they say it's all right for you to call them by their first name. In my own practice, I call everyone by their last name—like Mr. Douglas or Mr. Connery—until I'm invited to use their first name. The same is true of professional titles. If somebody has *Dr.* in front of their name, or a title, *definitely* call them by their title. Speaking from experience, when someone goes through eight to ten years of pain and torture to get their degree they certainly deserve all the respect that goes with the obligations of the title.

People often come into my office and ask, "Do I have to call you Dr. Glass?" Usually I will say, "You can call me whatever you feel comfortable with. 'Lillian' is fine." However, in specific professional situations where my title is an asset if somebody introduces me as Ms. Glass, I will correct them by saying it's "Dr. Glass."

All of this comes down to one word—RESPECT. One of the most important things missing in the way we greet each other in our society is respect. One of my clients, Vera, is the most popular teller at a bank where she has worked for over thirty years. Vera's line is always the longest because she treats every customer with respect and dignity. She looks right at them and speaks to them and never fails to call them by their name and title. "Thank you, Dr. Jones," Vera will say, or "How are you today, Mrs. Reed?" People love Vera's special attention so much that when the bank manager tells the customers that there is a shorter line at another teller's window, most of the customers will ignore it and say, "That's okay, I'll just wait for Vera."

Vera is an example of how people are literally willing to wait in line to be addressed with respect.

TITLES YOU NEED TO KNOW

We all need to know what to call people with titles in the event that we come in contact with them socially or professionally, from religious leaders and college professors to judges and politicians. Titles can be confusing so here is a list of some important titles you may have to use sometimes in your life.

Religious Leaders

In the Roman Catholic church, Priests are called "Father"; Bishops and Archbishops are called "Your Excellency" or "Bishop"; Cardinals are called "Your Eminence" or "Cardinal," while the Pope is addressed as "Your Holiness" or "Most Holy Father."

Some Protestant denominations also have Bishops, as well as Deans, Archdeacons, and Canons. All Protestant clergy, men and women, with doctoral degrees are addressed as "Doctor" or "Reverend." Protestant clergy without a doctoral degree are addressed as "Reverend."

In the Jewish faith, all Rabbis are addressed as "Rabbi," and Cantors, both men and women, are "Cantor."

Academicians

If you are taking to a *Professor*, his or her title is either "Professor," or "Doctor" if they have a Ph.D. If you are talking to the *Dean* or the *President* of the college or university, the correct title is "Dean" or "President."

Lawyers and Judges

All *Lawyers* are addressed simply as "Mr.," "Mrs.," or "Ms.," unless they happen to be a *Judge*, in which case they are called "Mr. Justice" or "Judge." Or more formally, "The Honorable Judge" and their last names. For example, The Honorable Judge Judith Stein.

Medical Professionals

All medical professionals—medical doctors, dentists, and doctors of veterinary medicine—should all be addressed as "Doctor."

Politicians

Mayors are "Mr. Mayor," or "Mayor," or "Madam Mayor."

All *state politicians* are addressed by their positions— "Secretary of State————."

Governors, both men and women, are all "Governor."

Ambassadors are "Ambassador," "Mr. Ambassador," or "Madam Ambassador."

Congressional representatives are introduced by "Representative," their name and the state which they are from; i.e., Representative Black from Kansas.

Senators are referred to as "Senator" in front of their name.

The *Speaker of the House of Representatives* is referred to as "Mr. Speaker" or "Madam Speaker."

The President's *Cabinet members* are "Mr. Secretary" or "Madam Secretary."

Supreme Court Justices are all called "Justice" regardless of their sex.

The *Vice President* is "Mr. Vice President,"or "Madam Vice President."

And finally, the *President of the United States* is addressed as "Mr. President" or "Madam President" (in the future).

NICKNAMES AND NAME CHANGES

Jeanie was a spunky, upbeat, charming girl who was like a ray of sunshine to the people who knew her. She just didn't feel like a Jeanie to her friends, so they nicknamed her "Sunshine." The name felt so good to Jeanie that she actually wound up legally changing her name to "Sunshine."

While nicknames can be an endearing way to address a person, it is not in your best interest to call someone by their nickname unless you're intimate with them or they've given you permission to call them by their nicknames. It's a matter of respect. For instance, Dustin Hoffman's nickname is "Dusty," but this is a name that he reserves for people he is close to. If you want to call someone by their nickname, don't be afraid to ask them, "May I call you 'Smiley'?" or "May I call you 'Bunny'?"

Above all, never make fun of another person's name. There are people with funny-sounding names, like Rip Torn or Candy

Cane or Pepper Steak, and you can be certain that these people have heard the joke before and aren't too thrilled about having fun made of their names. So show them the respect they deserve and take their name as seriously as they do.

If you don't like your own name, change it or take on a nickname. We've all heard the expression, "What's in a name?" Well, there's a lot in a name because your name reflects *you* and who *you* are.

You don't have to be an actor seeking a new image for yourself to change your name. If you are embarrassed by your name or nickname, or if it has been like an albatross around your neck all of your life, change it.

Julian, a client of mine, did. He hated his name. He hated people thinking he was a woman, calling him Julianne and getting letters to Mrs. or Ms. Stoller instead of Mr. Stoller. So he changed his name to Jeff. People insisted on calling him Julian after he changed his name, but he politely corrected them by saying "My name is Jeff."

For years, Robert Lamb, one of the lead singers in the singing group Chicago, was known as Bobby Lamb—until one day when he decided to change his name to Robert. He simply realized that he had gone through a complete metamorphosis. He had grown up and become a father with three children and a wife, and he decided he wanted to change his name to a more appropriate one for him. Bobby represented his past—Robert is his present. Now he is Robert, and says that he feels like a Robert, like an adult and not like the Bobby of his past. If you feel uncomfortable with your name, don't be afraid to change it.

On the other hand, if you are comfortable with your name, everyone else will be, too. For instance, many people used to make fun of the name Sylvester, until Sylvester Stallone made it into a great name to have.

It is up to you to feel good about your name, and if you don't, it's up to you to free yourself of your name and rename yourself.

CULTURAL GREETINGS

Having a fear of meeting and greeting people can even be the result of cultural differences. In our mobile world, we come in contact with people from different cultures and we may give the wrong impression unknowingly. We may find people from certain cultures cold, stand-offish, aloof, or even overly effusive.

If you are unaware what the greeting etiquette is in a certain culture, you can definitely get the wrong impression, which could in turn curtail your relationship with a person.

In order to properly greet people from a specific culture, you need to make it your business to learn about the culture. This will not only bring about more respect, but you will have an easier time communicating with the person.

In order to help you learn how to better meet and greet people from various cultures, here is a chart that tells you how people from different cultures greet one another.

GREETINGS ACROSS THE WORLD

Country	Greeting
AFRICA	• Handshake, formal greeting, "hello" • Avoid "Hi."
AUSTRALIA	• Use first names • Warm handshake • Wave (from a distance) • Men are termed "mate" to friends.
AUSTRIA	• Greet people whether they are strangers or not
BELGIUM	• Shake hands • Quick handshake • Woman offers hand first • Close friends kiss on cheek
BRITISH ISLES	• Handshakes and "hello" • Titles are used to show respect

CANADA/UNITED STATES	• Firm handshake • Sincere "hello" • Physical contact among close friends • Titles
CENTRAL AMERICA	• *"Abrazo"* or hug common greeting between friends • Women kiss each other on both cheeks to say hello and goodbye
CHINA/TAIWAN/HONG KONG	• Use full name and title • Last name is said first
FIJI	• Smile and upward flinch of eyebrows • Touch when talking • Handshakes • Use first names
FRANCE	• Single, quick handshake with slight pressure in grip when greeting and departing • Woman always offers hand first in handshake
GREECE	• Handshake • Warm greeting with embrace and both cheeks kissed • Slapping hand at shoulder level for close friends
HUNGARY/ROMANIA/ BULGARIA/POLAND/ CZECHOSLOVAKIA	• Handshake • Titles • Greetings for close friends • First names for young people • Close friends and relatives receive a kiss on both cheeks
INDIA	• *Namaste*—bend head gently with palms together below chin • No touching women

ISRAEL	• Warm handshakes • Pat on back • First names usually used • Titles unimportant • "Shalom" used to say hello and goodbye
JAPAN	• Bowing to greet—the lower the bow, the more respect • Return bow for as long and low as the other person is bowing • Use titles • Business cards exchanged after introduction
KOREA	• Slight bow with handshake • Two-handed handshake or right-handed handshake • Complete attention is paid to person being greeted
MALAYSIA	• Handshake only between men • Slight bow or head nod for elders • No handshaking with the elderly • Close male friends grasp both hands of each other
MIDDLE EAST	• First names only among close friends • Titles important • Handshakes • Kisses on cheek for men
NEW ZEALAND	• Polite, formal-greeting phrases, such as, "How do you do?" • Always use titles • Handshaking • Women offer hand first

PAKISTAN	• Handshake
	• Men don't shake hands with women
	• Use title and last name
PORTUGAL	• Sincere smile
	• Firm handshake
	• Titles used unless close friend
SINGAPORE	• Handshake with addition of slight bow
	• Titles used
SOUTH AMERICA	• Warm, cheerful greeting phrases such as *abrazos* (hugs)
	• Hugs and embraces
	• Kissing on one cheek
	• Titles used
	• Shaking hands with slight inclination of head, which shows respect
	• Only use first name when invited to do so
	• Children are kissed and arms put around shoulders
SOVIET UNION	• Handshake with slight bow to show respect
	• Stating name with handshake only when meeting someone new instead of "Hello"
	• For people you know, three kisses on the cheek and hugging
SPAIN	• Handshake for men and women
	• Hug only if friends haven't seen each other for a while
	• Titles always used until one is well acquainted

- First names if close friends only
- *Don* and *Doña* with first name show respect

SWITZERLAND
- Handshake
- Polite, formal-greeting phrases even among strangers
- Titles and family names used except with close friends

THAILAND
- No handshaking
- *Wai* used where both hands are placed together in prayer position at chest and bowing slightly
- Higher hands, more respect
- Always return *Wai*, which means "I'm sorry," "Hello," or "Thank you."
- Use first names only

A few years ago, the Pope came to America and created such a positive impression not only because of his spirituality, but because of how he touched everyone he came in contact with. His greetings transcended all cultural barriers as people felt something very personal emanating from him. He looked at people directly and with wide-open eyes, literally, with each person who came into his path.

The Pope is an extraordinary person, gifted with a selflessness that enables him to give himself completely to others. We can all learn from this very special person about how to be open when communicating with others.

Even if you feel you have all of life's burdens on your shoulders, you owe it to other human beings to treat them with the respect and dignity they deserve, to get out of your problems for a moment and connect with them. Once you start to really connect with others, you will be surprised at your ability to relate to other people. All of us can do this by starting out with the basics of knowing how to effectively greet others.

... 2 ...

Being a Good Conversationalist

A great conversationalist is someone who connects with people and makes them feel important, like Vera, the bank teller mentioned in the previous chapter. Warren Beatty is one of the best communicators in Hollywood. When he talks to you, he makes you feel like you're the only person in the room, which is probably why he is so successful with women. Edward James Olmos, Academy–Award nominee for *Stand and Deliver*, is another gifted communicator. I had the good fortune to work with him when he was playing the part of a gypsy in a movie called *Triumph of the Spirit*. He has a gift for making everyone around him feel important by treating them with respect.

Actress Marlee Matlin is a truly amazing communicator, and she's deaf. She makes you feel like you're the only person in the room. In addition, Marlee is so physically expressive when she communicates. I adore working with deaf people because they are so communicative through their facial expressions. Hearing-people can learn much about good communication from watching deaf people communicate.

Becoming a good conversationalist requires knowing how to *start a conversation*, how to *keep it going*, and *how to end a conversation*. The rest of this chapter will show you how to be the *best* conversationalist you can be.

STARTING A CONVERSATION

Starting a conversation usually means coming up with an opening line, or "icebreaker." The best kind of icebreaker is one that is positive—after all, the last thing people want to hear from a stranger is how noisy the party is, how awful the food is, or how ugly the people are dressed.

A compliment is always a great icebreaker. If you feel like saying to someone, "You look great in that dress," it will usually be appreciated. Sometimes you may want to be more subtle— "That's a very unusual belt. Did you buy it in this country?" It pays to be observant of the other person.

You may even want to wear something unusual yourself to a gathering—something other people can comment on in order to break the ice with you.

"Doesn't Judy throw terrific parties?" is a good way to break the ice because it leaves the other person room for a "positive space" to respond.

Any news event is a good ice breaker. I encourage all of my clients to read the newspaper or listen to the news on the radio or television, because it is so important for all of us to know what is going on in the world. There are more informative publications, television newscasts, and radio newscasts available today than ever before, so it is unacceptable to be ill-informed in this day and age. Reading *USA Today* or watching "Headline News" on CNN is one of the quickest ways to get the days events as they both capsulize everything with vivid visuals. No matter what your way of getting the news is, I can't stress enough how important it is for all of us to be well-informed, especially if we are busy meeting new people.

The weather is another a great opener. Many a relationship has begun with, "Wonderful weather we're having." This is an obvious overture to a conversation, and how the other person picks up on it is a good indication of whether they are interested in having a conversation with you or whether it would be in your best interest to find someone more receptive to talk to.

The fact is, any opening line will do, as long as it is not negative, and as long as it is not a "line." "Lines" are turnoffs. No one wants to hear an obvious line like "How does it feel to be the best-looking person in this room?" The best way to entice a person to have a conversation with you is by being sincere and respectful and letting them know that you are interested in talking to them.

KEEPING THE CONVERSATION GOING

Once you've got a conversation going, the best way to keep it going is by asking the other person questions that don't require just a "yes" or "no" answer, or questions that show genuine interest on your part as you hear what they have to say. For example, if someone says:

"I'm from Miami," you may respond with: "Oh, I've been to Miami," and continue with: "How long have you lived there?" Them: "I was born there and have lived there all my life." You: "That's unusual. Most people go there to vacation. I've never met anyone who was a native. Is your family from Miami as well?" Them: "Yes. I'm a fourth-generation Miamian."

As you can see by this conversation, you need to keep asking questions based on the last thing a person says. In essence, elaborate on what *they* just said and ask them more about it. This is called the "Elaboration Technique." This technique is also what a good reporter learns to do in order to get a good interview.

THE ELABORATION TECHNIQUE

When you are asking a person questions, choose questions that will get the person to elaborate on what they are saying. Act like a reporter and ask them questions without becoming too intrusive. Ask questions similar to those a reporter might ask to draw a person out—*who, what, when, where,* and *why* questions. For example:

You: "What's your favorite type of food?"

Them: "I love Italian food."

You: "Well, I'll tell you, last week I went to the best Italian restaurant ever. Do you like veal parmesan?"

Them: "Yes, I do."

You: "Well, they prepared it so well. It was as good as any

restaurant I've been in when I visited Italy. Have you ever been to Italy?"

Once you hit on something you find interesting, keep asking questions in order to get the other person to elaborate on the topic as much as possible. A good conversationalist elaborates on the experiences they have had.

Instead of saying Lisa's party was fun, tell *why* it was fun. Describe *why* you had a good time—who was there, what happened, where it was, and how she arranged the party. Go into more detail when describing the party.

Description is the best form of communication, because it keeps peoples' interest up and stimulates them. Use words to create images and paint pictures so that the other person can get a visual as well as auditory image of what you are describing to them. For example: "It was the most fabulous and unique party. A band dressed in white tuxedo tails played authentic music from the 1920s. The entire room was decorated in art deco, which is my favorite period, and everyone wore black and white formal wear. There were tuber roses and calla lilies and gardenias, which made the room smell so wonderful. They had a phenomenal ice sculpture in the middle of the room in the shape of a 1920s flapper. The detail of this ice sculpture was incredible—the face of the sculpture even resembled the hostess. The food was out of this world and was prepared by a chef who studied at the Cordon Bleu in Paris." If you use description effectively, you can even make the person feel as though they were actually there, too.

BE A GOOD OBSERVER AND REACTOR

Being a good *observer* and *reactor* means being attentive and sensitive to the other person's cues, both in their facial and body language. For example, if you ask somebody if their parents are living in the area and they frown or back off slightly, their visual cues show that you've probably touched a sensitive subject area for them. Perhaps they lost a family member or perhaps they aren't on good terms with their parents, or maybe they feel it's simply none of your business—that you've been too intrusive.

Look for eye contact cues. If the other person is constantly looking away, they may be interested in something or someone else, in which case you can either say, "You seem preoccupied," or you take their cue and wind up the conversation and leave. Paying attention to a person's visual cues can tell you as much as or even more than what they say verbally.

PERSONALIZE YOUR COMMENTS

When you are having a conversation with another person, ask questions and respond to their answers by adding personalized comments. Then ask another question that relates to your personalized comment. Example: "Oh, you're from Colorado? I go to Aspen every winter. I just love it. Have you ever spent any time in Aspen?" After you make a personal comment about the answer, ask another question as it relates to your personal comment. This is called *mutual conversation.* Don't just give personal comments that turn into a soliloquy as this will oftentimes bore the other person.

For example, don't do this: "Oh, I love Colorado, I love to ski in the winter, and I love to go fishing in the mountain lakes during the summer. I'm even thinking of buying a place in Aspen if I can ever get the money together. It's just that I bought this new car this year, and my condo payments . . ."

This is a total turnoff. Instead, you need to give a little information, ask a question, wait for the answer, and then respond again.

I recently conducted a survey among my clients and asked them to write down what they found most annoying when having a conversation with a person. The number-one turnoff from almost everyone was listening to a person go on and on about themselves. People are offended by those who constantly use the word "I" and never listen to the other person. Nobody likes a narcissist.

TIPS FOR MAINTAINING A GOOD CONVERSATION

In order to keep a good conversation going, here are seven tips that can help you be an excellent communicator:

1. *Be aware of your own body and facial language.* Good body language means making good facial contact when you speak, not invading the other person's space, and being physically expressive without being *excessive.* In the next chapter you will find specific exercises to help rid yourself of excessive gesturing.

2. *Don't gossip.* Whenever you start gossiping, you run the risk of offending the person you are talking to because of their possible relationship to the person being gossiped about. It also makes you look small, so don't be a part of it.

3. *Cultivate a wide range of topics.* I can't stress enough how important it is that you keep up with current events by reading newspapers and magazines so that you can discuss a variety of subjects. When you are talking to someone you do not know very well, it is probably best to stay away from politics and religion or anything controversial at first.

4. *Have a sense of humor.* Everyone enjoys a humorous story or joke. Even though sexual and ethnic humor oftentimes gets a laugh or a chuckle, it's not worth the effect that the jokes may have on your "total image." People may be offended by your humor, which may in turn reflect poor judgment on your part and may encourage them to think less of you.

5. *Don't interrupt.* As a communications specialist I have conducted numerous surveys asking people what qualities they are most irritated by during conversations. Close to ninety-five percent of the people surveyed say they hate being interrupted. If you want to be a good conversationalist, you need to fight the impulse to interrupt and give the person you are talking to the time they need to complete what they are saying to you. Just keep taking your breath in and *hold* your breath as well as your tongue, then slowly let out the air as you wait until the other person finishes what they have to say.

6. *Be enthusiastic and upbeat.* Don't be afraid to show enthusiasm and use positive re-enforcement whenever possible. Your enthusiasm allows the other person to feel that you are interested in what they are saying to you. Later on in the book, you will find a series of exercises to help you learn to

become more animated and use more emotion when talking and listening.

7. *Be flexible in your point of view.* Always try to be as open as possible and try to see things from the other person's point of view. You certainly can express your own views, but express them in a way that is not hostile, offensive, or defensive.

ENDING A CONVERSATION

If you've started a conversation with another person and you're having difficulty ending it, there are subtle signals you can send to the other person that will bring the conversation to its close without hurting anyone's feelings.

Breaking eye contact is a good way of signaling to the other person that you are ready to end the conversation. Assuming that you have maintained good eye contact throughout the conversation, looking off in another direction is a discreet signal that the conversation is about to end.

Another way to signal that a conversation is coming to an end is to use transition words like "Well" or "At any rate" or even use statements like "It was really nice talking to you." You may then want to recap all that was said. To recap, look at the other person and state key points that have been made—theirs and yours—and express your appreciation for their point of view. Then you may add, "I've really enjoyed talking to you. I hope we will have a chance to have another conversation soon."

Whatever you do, don't lie to the other person. If you are not interested in talking to them again, don't mention the possibility of a future meeting just to be polite. That is hypocritical. Instead, you may want to say "Nice meeting you" and then leave.

When you leave, it's essential to end on a strong note vocally by projecting your voice and using proper inflection so that you leave a positive impression. Finally, be sure to give the other person a good, firm handshake. The final impression you make can be just as important as the initial impression you made.

... 3 ...

Winning Friends in the 90s

It has been over half a century since Dale Carnegie wrote his famous book *How to Win Friends and Influence People*. Since then, over 30 million Americans have purchased and read this best-selling book whose principles are still being taught in hundreds of Dale Carnegie courses throughout the country to date.

Even though Dale Carnegie had a great vision at the time, his book was written at a time in history in which we must question whether it is as relevant *today* as it was over fifty years ago.

Yesterday's bible of how-to-communicate may not be relevant for modern-day communicators. Since the book was written, three wars have taken place, the economy has skyrocketed, and the communication revolution with advances in computer-technology telecommunication has taken place. Satellites now beam live information from all parts of the world right into our own homes through our most advanced television systems. Values, morals, attitudes, styles, and acceptable behavior have also changed drastically.

Today people are so much more educated, so much more aware, and much more sophisticated than they were in Mr. Carnegie's day, when only the privileged few had a higher education. Today, almost anyone has the opportunity to get a university education and higher degrees. People also tend to be more inclined today toward self-discovery and sexual openness.

While some of Dale Carnegie's ideas may still ring true after so much change has taken place in society, many of the ideas are outdated and aren't appropriate for communicating in the 90s.

For example, in his book Mr. Carnegie tells us to *Talk in terms of the other man's interests.*

First of all, we are no longer a society of men. Women now share an equally prominent place in all areas of society, especially in the world of business.

And second, although showing interest in the other person's interests may be a good way to get people to open up to you, doing too much of this is often construed as being phoney or patronizing. Today, good communication is a give-and-take proposition where *both* people need to speak *mutually* of their interests.

Dale Carnegie says: *Remember that a man's name is to him the sweetest and most important sound in any language.*

It certainly is a good idea to repeat a person's name *from time to time* during a conversation, since that is part of the "branding" process—getting someone's identity ingrained in your mind so that you don't forget it.

Using a person's name in a conversation can also be an attention-getting device when important points are made. However, if you constantly use the person's name throughout the conversation, the technique will lose its potency or effectiveness as an attention-getting device and will become more of an annoyance. This can also impede what you are trying to get across.

Dale Carnegie says: *Never tell a man he is wrong.*

I don't believe that this is very good advice. You have to maintain your integrity and not be a hypocrite. Withholding information or having a *don't-make-waves* attitude can only get you into trouble today. You build up ill feelings and harbor them. In today's world, being a good communicator means being open, honest, and direct—yet tactful.

There are ways of telling someone they are wrong without destroying them: "I can appreciate what you're saying, but my thoughts on the matter are different." Sometimes, no matter how tactful you are, there are some people that just don't listen. In that case, you may need to blatantly yet politely tell them what your feelings are and how you feel they are mistaken.

Dale Carnegie says: *If you are wrong, admit it quickly and emphatically.*

How can a philosophy that doesn't allow you to tell another person that *they* are wrong require you to "admit quickly and emphatically" if *you* are wrong—or if you think you may be wrong? Is it really in your best interest to be so quick to reject your own points of view?

Granted, it is a good idea to admit you're wrong; however, it's important to know how to admit you're wrong in order to "save face" and not lose your credibility. Instead of using the quick and emphatic Dale Carnegie approach, you might say, "You know, I've given it some thought and I can really see what you're saying," as opposed to blurting out, "I was wrong, you are right." It's important to admit you're wrong, but don't be overly hostile to yourself by saying such things as "How stupid of me," or "What a dummy I am." You need to be as sensitive and understanding of yourself in admitting you're wrong as you would be to the other person.

According to Dale Carnegie, to win people to your way of thinking you should *Get the other person saying "Yes, Yes" immediately.*

What if he or she isn't ready to jump on your bandwagon and say "yes" right away? Just because a person says "yes" once doesn't mean they necessarily agree with everything else you say. People today are too sophisticated to be taken in by this kind of manipulation. If you try to manipulate someone, you usually risk losing their trust. The best way to win someone over to your way of thinking is to communicate your ideas to them honestly, directly, and openly in a non-defensive tone.

Dale Carnegie says: *Let the other man do a great deal of the talking.*

Ideally, a conversation should be a fifty-fifty sharing experience for both of the participants, which "includes" you as well. A good way to draw the person out and have them participate is to ask them questions that get an exchange going so that there is a fifty-fifty exchange, with people sharing thoughts, feelings, and expressions.

Dale Carnegie says: *Let the other fellow feel the idea is his.*

This is unacceptable. It is phoney and dishonest. If you come up with an idea, it's yours. You need to own it. You should never let them think your idea is theirs just to get them enthusiastic about something. This is manipulative and not what today's communication is all about.

Dale Carnegie says: *Begin with praise and appreciation.*

I agree that a little praise can go a long way if it's sincere. However, the problem is too much praise can become patronizing, and can be interpreted as insincere. It often encourages falseness that is simply meant to get on someone's good side or to "butter them" up for the negativity you are about to let them have. If your praise is overly effusive, it may even cause people to question what you want from them. If you are going to say something negative to someone, be direct and forthright. You don't have to couch it with niceness or sugarcoat it.

Dale Carnegie says: *Call attention to people's mistakes indirectly.*

I completely disagree with this advice. The direct and honest approach is the best way to confront people. If you're going to call attention to a mistake a person has made, it's in everyone's best interest to confront the person *honestly* and *directly*. Oftentimes when someone is indirect, the person who made the mistake may not "get" it, and they make the mistake again. The result is you may harbor resentment toward them, so you need to be upfront and directly confront their mistake.

Dale Carnegie says: *Talk about your own mistakes before criticizing the other person.*

This philosophy takes for granted that people cannot accept criticism without some kind of sugar coating. Don't criticize yourself just to make the person feel comfortable. That is patronizing and unacceptable behavior.

Dale Carnegie says: *Praise the slightest improvement and praise every improvement. Be hearty in your approbation and lavish in your praise.*

Most people interpret lavish praise as phoney and insincere. Although it's good to acknowledge how well a person is doing with a weight-loss program, praising the fact that they ate vegetables and no dessert and had no wine at dinner whenever you go out with them can be unnerving. Praising the slightest and every improvement can be annoying. You run the risk of not being taken seriously.

In the last fifty years, Dale Carnegie was a catalyst for showing people how to be more effective communicators and how to better fit into society. However, these Depression-era teachings can no longer be the doctrine of the 90s because times have changed. Women's rights, civil rights, and human rights are becoming realities. We now live in a time where Oprah Winfrey, Phil Donahue, and Geraldo Rivera discuss the most intimate subjects right in our living rooms. Ours is a society where very little is censored and where our First-Amendment right—freedom of speech—is of paramount importance. Everything and everyone is open for discussion as we enter the twenty-first century in which there is a new set of rules by which to win friends and influence people.

CONFIDENCE THROUGH COMPLIMENTS

When I was about ten years old, somebody paid me a compliment that has stayed with me my whole life. I was a bucktoothed little girl who went to my orthodontist on a monthly basis to have my braces tightened. Dr. Bernard Geltzer would say to me, "One day you're going to be so pretty that we're not going to know what to do with you." The next time I came in, Dr. Geltzer would say, "Let's see that Miss-America smile." Even though he didn't realize it, his compliments made me feel attractive and important. He contributed much to my self-esteem as a child. "You know, Lillian," he said, as I ran into him in my adult years, "I always knew you were a beauty."

Everyone needs compliments and positive strokes in order to thrive and be the best they can be.

Most people who are extremely successful in life have come from families that believed in them—who were not afraid to tell them how great they were even into adulthood. Usually, if you give honest and sincere compliments to the people around you, you'll find that they will be more receptive to you and will want to be around you.

When we are small children, the praise and the compliments we get from our parents is the nourishment that enables our self-esteem to thrive and grow. But for some reason, most of us seem to stop getting praise and compliments as we get older. Usually when we become pre-teens. How come we are no longer so cute and clever? What was cute at five or six is ignored at ten or eleven. Why should these compliments stop all of a sudden? How come we're not getting compliments telling us that we're so cute or that we're such a good artist like we did when we were younger? Now we hear, "Don't get so big-headed," or "Don't let it go to your head" when we say "Don't I look pretty today?" or "Isn't this a beautiful picture I painted?"

So many of us don't know how to accept compliments because we have been programmed not to build ourselves up, not to get "big-headed." When others try to build us up we find it difficult to accept the compliments.

Some ignore the compliment (as if nothing was said), others downplay it, still others joke about it, and some others blush out of embarrassment. All these responses reflect discomfort at being complimented. How well you accept a compliment tells a great deal about your self-esteem and how you feel about yourself.

GETTING PEOPLE TO ACCEPT YOUR COMPLIMENTS

If someone can't or won't accept your compliment, you need to keep reassuring them of your sincerity. Getting people to take your compliments more seriously can be as easy as putting more emotion and sincerity into your voice. So many people deliver compliments so flatly, with such a lack of enthusiasm and emotion, that you may doubt their sincerity.

If your voice is textured with genuine human emotion, people will respond more favorably toward you. So put life into your tones as you compliment and let your praises flow freely. Just look the person in the eye and compliment them from the heart.

Let the praises flow openly and don't be stingy. If you think someone is great, let them know it. If someone delivers a speech that touches you, give them the same good feeling back. For example, "I've heard a lot of speakers and I have to tell you— you are the best speaker I have ever heard. Your speech moved me to tears."

Giving someone a sincere and honest compliment is the best gift you can give. It's a gift you need to give freely.

A NOTE IS WORTH A THOUSAND WORDS

When you feel special toward a person, you may want to do more than just say "thank you." You may want to express your feelings of gratitude in writing. This further "brands" how you feel about a person. Keep a stack of thank-you cards by your desk, and when people affect you in a special way, send them a note.

Research shows that women write more thank-you notes than men because they tend to be taught to do this early on in life. However, many successful men write notes regularly, and it has a positive effect on their interpersonal relationships. Superagent Norman Brokaw is President and CEO of the William Morris talent agency and one of the most communicative individuals I've ever met. He constantly writes notes to people, congratulating them on a specific project or for winning an award. This endears him to others as they think of him in a positive way.

If someone has touched you, why not share with them how they have affected your life? Even if you don't know them, the gesture will be appreciated. Doing this can help cement budding friendships as well as add more tender feelings to existing ones. Everybody wants a sincere compliment that acknowledges their achievements.

It doesn't take much to drop someone a note and let them know how much you appreciate them and how much they mean to you.

GIVING *YOURSELF* A VERBAL PAT ON THE BACK

When you've done something you're proud of, don't be afraid to let others know about it. Sharing this positive information with them gives them further insight into who you are and allows them to get to know you a little better.

A couple of years ago, a dermatologist friend of mine told me a story about how he had been to a party and saw a woman with a suspicious-looking mole on her neck. After a few minutes of polite conversation, he asked her if she had seen a doctor about the mole. She said she hadn't noticed it and it was probably nothing to worry about. He told her that he was a doctor and that the mole looked suspicious and invited her to come to his office so that he could do a biopsy. She came to see him and was glad she did when she discovered that her mole was a life-threatening melanoma. In essence, the doctor's persistence, openness, and honesty had saved this woman's life. The doctor was not proud of his correct diagnosis but of his persistence and his tenacity and his refusal to take "no" for an answer when a person's life was at stake. By sharing this story with me and giving himself a well-deserved pat on the back, he further validated the respect and admiration I had for him as a physician and as a person.

Another person who shared their pride with me was Cecilia Bolocco, the former Miss Chile and Miss Universe, with whom I recently served as judge in the Miss USA Pageant. Cecilia told us that she had always felt awkward about all the attention she received as Miss Universe. However, her greatest moment while holding the Miss Universe title was when she used her title to help Chilean flood victims. She used her position to organize a special telethon to help the people whose lives had been destroyed by the flood and she raised large sums of money for the relief victims. Cecilia's story showed she was as beautiful a person on the inside as she was on the outside.

There is nothing wrong with patting yourself on the back. It can enhance your total image.

MAKING OTHERS FEEL IMPORTANT

If you want to make a good impression on people and maintain a good relationship, you need to give others respect and enable them to feel important when they are around you.

There are people who are gifted when it comes to making

others feel important, and the magic of their success is their ability to make a person feel like they are the one person in the room. Warren Beatty, whom I mentioned earlier, and George Hamilton are two people who have the ability to make a woman feel as though she is the only person in the room. Former President Ronald Reagan and Barbara Walters are other gifted communicators who are sensitive to making others feel important, and their communication skills have obviously served them well. These high-level communicators have the ability to make others feel important because they give the person they are speaking with complete attention. They use eye contact and facial animation, they have warm and approachable posture and body language, and are genuinely interested in what the other person has to say.

GOOD COMMUNICATION REQUIRES A GOOD MEMORY

Being a good communicator requires having a good memory and remembering things about the other person. Doesn't it make you feel special when you haven't seen someone in a while and they remember something you never thought they would remember—like how your dog is doing since he had that bad reaction to his distemper shot, or how you enjoyed your trip to Hawaii several months ago? If you really want to attract people and maintain good, solid relationships, you need to be a good "rememberer." It's something that doesn't come easy for many. In fact, you have to train yourself and constantly work at it.

So many of my clients are amazed at how much I remember from our sessions. One woman whom I hadn't seen in ten years dropped by my office one day just to say hello, and I asked her, "Did you ever get rid of that awful boss you had?" The man, who had tormented her for years with his demands and his horrible temper, had finally been transferred to another office. My client was amazed I had been able to remember the details of her awful experience.

Very often people comment on my "extraordinary memory," but, in actuality, my "secret" is that I genuinely care about people and care about what they say to me. I make a special effort to remember the things they share with me. I do this by visualization. I create pictures in my mind while they are talking to me.

If someone tells me about a trip they took to the Caribbean, I will picture them fishing. I will see them in a boat hauling in a big fish out of the clear blue tropical water. I will brand that image in my mind, and later, when I see them again, I will be able to ask them, "How was your trip? Did you catch any fish?" I did this visualization technique with actor Herve Villechaize, a former client who played Tattoo on "Fantasy Island." Herve was amazed when I started recalling the details of the ranch that he had described to me several years earlier—right down to the chicks and pigs that I had visualized being fed by him. You can do this as well. It's easy and will endear you to people for "caring" enough to remember. If you want to improve your memory, you have to get unself-absorbed.

The next time you talk to one of your friends, or even a new acquaintance, try to visualize and auditorize everything they are telling you. Try to create pictures in as much detail as possible in your mind so that you brand images in your brain.

Try to go beyond the visual. Use all of your senses. Get involved in the taste, the smell, and the feel of what is being described. You need to incorporate all of your senses when you paint your visual pictures.

BEING APPROACHABLE

Oftentimes, if you have an approachable manner about you, people will respond to you and be attracted to you like a magnet. Approachability involves your body posture, gestures, and your facial expression.

Being Too Rigid

Being too rigid can detract from a positive impression. Stuart, a businessman client of mine, made everyone terribly nervous because of his extremely rigid voice and manner. He literally choked the words out of his mouth, and his body movements were so painfully stiff and awkward that he was almost robotic.

He made people feel that he was just too uptight to communicate with anyone.

Through physical relaxation exercises, I taught him to be more flexible in his body movements, which in turn made people feel more comfortable around him. The result was that he noticed a definite improvement in his business and in his interpersonal relationships.

Don't Be Too Casual

Just as being too rigid can be a turnoff, so can being too casual. Having a sloppy, casual posture can give someone the wrong impression. In fact, studies have shown that you can sabotage yourself with bad posture. One hundred people were shown photographs of people with bad posture (head down, shoulders rounded, stomach out) and photographs of people with good posture (head up, shoulders back), and the people with poor posture were consistently judged to be less popular, less exciting, less ambitious, less friendly and less intelligent than their counterparts with good posture. If your posture is too stiff, you will communicate uptightness, like Stuart did, while too loose a posture can communicate sloppiness and carelessness. A hunched-over back communicates a lack of confidence and self-respect. By simply straightening out your shoulders and holding your head up, you can significantly change people's impressions of you.

Frances, a thirty-five-year-old advertising account executive, came to me because she had just taken a new job with an agency and she wasn't getting the respect she needed from her new creative team.

The moment I met Frances, I could tell exactly what her problem was—she had terrible posture. She stood and walked like she was timid, with her shoulders rounded and her head bent down. Her posture seemed to say "I have no self-respect, so you don't need to respect me either."

By holding her head up by an imaginary string and rotating her shoulders back, Frances was able to improve her posture dramatically. With her new posture she exuded a newfound confidence, and she even observed that people, especially her creative team, treated her with the respect she deserved and even approached her for advice more often than they previously did.

APPROACHABLE FACIAL APPEARANCE

All too often when someone is concentrating intensely or thinking about something, their face will show an expression that doesn't reflect who they are or what they are thinking about. For example, a furrowed brow and a squinty-eyed facial expression when you are "thinking" may be misinterpreted as your being angry or hostile or mean. So if you are in the presence of others you need to be "mindful" of your facial expression at all times.

It may not even be a bad idea to keep a mirror near your desk at work so you can see how you come across. This will help you monitor your body, head, and facial movements throughout the day. Having a friend or family member remind you when you are committing one of your bad facial habits can also be very helpful. Just make sure you tell them to point it out subtly and positively, not with harassment or negativity.

Another way to relax tense facial muscles is to every hour or so make yourself aware of what parts of your face are feeling tense. Then close your eyes and take a mini-vacation for a few seconds. Picture yourself in your fantasy environment, relaxed and calm. Think great thoughts! Keeping your eyes closed, imagine all tension leaving your forehead, eyes, nose, cheeks, upper and lower lips, jaw, ears, and neck. Usually when you open your eyes you are relaxed. Others will now see an approachable person to talk to.

Just as inappropriate facial animation can confuse people and turn them off, too little facial expression can also be a turnoff. If you want to have more honest and meaningful relationships with other people and win their confidence, you need to start wearing your emotions on your face and not be afraid to expose your true feelings. For example, don't be afraid to express your emotions—sadness, surprise, anger, happiness, fear, disgust, compassion/sympathy, love, doubt, and boredom facially as well as vocally.

DEVELOPING GOOD TALKING HABITS

Besides having good body and facial language, better relationships with others require having good talking habits.

Research has shown that the way we sound greatly determines what people think of us. I have spent years teaching people to improve their speaking skills. This is dealt with in great depth in my book *Talk to Win*. My experiences have shown me that virtually anyone can improve their talking skills if they do the following: 1) open their mouths wide enough, 2) open the backs of their throats when they talk, 3) take a breath through their mouths, hold it for a second or two, and then speak on the exhalation, 4) draw out their vowel sounds to help slow down, 5) bear down and out on abdominal muscles in order to project the voice, and finally 6) put emotional meaning into what they are saying. These six steps can help reduce a too nasal-sounding voice, lower a high-pitched voice, slow you down, and put more life in what you say by giving you more vocal confidence. In essence, having a good speaking voice not only makes you more approachable but more likeable.

IF YOU DON'T HAVE ANYTHING POSITIVE TO SAY

In order for people to better relate to you, you need to limit how much negativity you spew forth. I have found in talking to people that "raining on someone's parade" or "popping their balloon" with negativity is a sure-fire way to lose friends and not succeed in any personal or business relationship. No one wants to hear why something *won't* work out. If they are sharing a dream with you, they need your support.

One of my clients couldn't understand why her daughter flew off the handle at her when she told her daughter to stop dreaming about being an artist and keep her secure job as a bank teller where she could meet nice men and make good money.

Instead, her daughter told her mother to "buzz off," and ended up quitting her job and eventually began supporting herself by drawing sketches of people outside a well-known restaurant during the evenings. She was able to make as much money working part-time doing sketches as she was able to make full-

time at the bank, and it freed her during the day to be creative
and paint. She devoted two full days a week to making contacts
in the art world, meeting with agents and gallery owners. Today Linda is an extremely successful artist in Los Angeles, *no*
thanks to her mother.

Because of her constant negativity, her mother wound up destroying her relationship with Linda. She might have been able
to share in her daughter's success by simply recognizing her
daughter's talent and being supportive.

A similar situation drove Giuseppe and Anthony apart. Anthony was an authoritarian man. He always knew best and always had to be in control of everything. Giuseppe was an Italian
immigrant who had trained as a tailor in Italy. When he arrived in America, he got a job in a large Los Angeles department store. Giuseppe was a very good tailor who was honest
and very hard-working, so it wasn't long before his loyal customers suggested that he start his own business. Excited about
this, he told his best friend, Anthony, about his plans. Anthony
was quick to express his negative opinions. He told Giuseppe
that he already had a good income and shouldn't take any
chances with a wife and child to support.

Giuseppe heard what his friend Anthony said, but he didn't
take his advice. Instead, he went to the bank, got a loan, bor-
rowed some more money from his customers, and opened up
his own tailor shop. His customers followed him, and within a
year Giuseppe had built a successful business. A couple of years
later, he bought a home and started bringing his relatives over
from Italy. When his next son was born, he didn't invite Anthony to the christening. There just wasn't room for Anthony's
negativity in Giuseppe's new life.

If somebody has a dream, it's in your best interest not to pop
it with your own limitations. If somebody tells you they want
to start a business, why badger them with how difficult it is, or
how many new businesses fail each year, or that they're blow-
ing it by leaving the security of their job? Being negative doesn't
endear you to others. The bottom line is, if you can't support
someone in their pipe dreams, don't say anything negative.

What do you do if someone comes to you with an idea that
sounds absolutely crazy—a woman who is five foot four, over-

weight, has a double chin, bad teeth, and mousy hair tells you she wants to become a fashion model?

You could say, "What, are you crazy?" and then with amazement watch her lose forty pounds, get her hair done, her teeth capped, and start modeling school. Or you might say, "That's wonderful. Good for you," or "If that's what you want, go for it," or "That's great, how are you going to go about it?" If you say any of these positive things, you'll most likely stay friends.

What do you say if someone has ambitions to lose weight? This is one of the most sensitive subjects facing us today. If someone says they want to lose weight, you're best off just being as supportive as you can. Damaged feelings—especially when it comes to weight control—are long to heal and are too often never forgotten.

Gina, who had always been very thin and attractive, had put on a lot of weight, to the point where she was disgusted with herself.

"I can't stand it anymore," she told her friend Marvin. "I don't know how I let myself get this much out of control. I've just got to lose this weight."

"I think you look great now," Marvin said. "I think you're gorgeous. But if you feel you would be more comfortable being thinner, I'll support you."

What a beautiful exchange! Marvin's support for Gina was entirely non-judgmental and without any personal prejudices. It was nothing like the response Gina got from her other friend, Jerry.

"It's about time you decided to take off the weight," Jerry had said. "You're way too heavy."

Then he proceeded to give her advice on where to go to work out, how to work out, what and what not to eat, and so on. In a word, he made her feel fat and unattractive.

"I want to see results from you," Jerry had said. Well, he saw results. He saw Gina shed fifty pounds, and he also saw that as part of her loss she shed their relationship. She never spoke to Jerry again.

The difference between Marvin's and Jerry's responses is that whereas Marvin was full of support, Jerry was full of judgment and advice. Whereas Jerry made Gina feel fat and unattractive,

Marvin made Gina feel attractive as a person, and she will never forget him.

It's not always so easy to be tactful. Sometimes you have to be blunt, but you can be tactfully blunt—you can be direct and honest so that the person will hear you, but mindful of that person's feelings.

LETTING SOMEONE KNOW THEY'VE OVERSTEPPED THEIR BOUNDS

There are times when someone may offer advice or make a comment about you in which they touch upon a sensitive nerve. They have said something to you that is literally "none of their business." What do you say to someone who has overstepped their bounds?

All too often people don't do anything about it! Even though they don't like the intrusion they accept the degradation. They don't say anything until it eats at them later on in the day. This "dig" or "invasive comment" or "advice" eats at them until they become angry and hostile. As they relive the verbal exchange in their mind they become angry at the person. They become even angrier at themselves for not telling the person that they should "mind their own business." They may even be angry with themselves for feeling as though they have to defend themselves. Not having an articulate comeback that would put the perpetrator back in his or her place can also cause a person to be very angry with himself or herself.

Jenna, a C.P.A., felt like kicking herself all afternoon as she mulled over in her mind what she should have said. When seated next to a male colleague at a business luncheon, he asked her "why she wasn't married." Jenna casually replied that she hadn't found Mr. Right yet. Her rude colleague immediately interjected, "Well, maybe you're just too picky. There is more to life than your job. You need to get out more so you can meet a husband."

At this point Jenna started feeling knots in her stomach. Her voice tightened and she could feel the tension in her neck. However, she managed to squeak out that she'd just been concentrating on her career. Her colleague then interjected, "Well, if you weren't such a workaholic, you could find time for a career and a husband."

At this point, Jenna had nothing else to say. All her insecurities started to bubble forth and she spoke as little as possible during the rest of the luncheon.

Instead of feeling bad and clamming up, Jenna should have taken the reins in hand and not allowed this conversation to get as far as it did. She should not have allowed her colleague to intimidate her. The moment she heard the question, "Why aren't you married?" she should have retorted, "Why do you ask?" After all, this was a professional situation, not a social one. Had her colleague said, "Oh, I'm just curious," she may have felt comfortable saying that she hadn't found Mr. Right yet. Had he persisted and accused her of being too "picky," she could have stopped the conversation immediately. She should have looked directly at her colleague, taken a breath in, and slowly said, "I find your comment about my being too picky inappropriate and I do not wish to discuss it with you."

By saying so, she lets her colleague know that she has limits and self-respect and that he has overstepped these limits. If her colleague is a gentleman, he will offer an apology and proceed to change the subject.

Often, when you tell someone they've overstepped their bounds, they will respect you more and you in turn will respect yourself even more. It's unfortunate, but most people have not yet learned when to stop asking invasive questions, so it's up to you to let them know your limit. You don't have to be hostile or aggressive or say something like "What's it to you?", "Mind your own business," or "Buzz off." Instead, you need to be tactful and allow the person to save face. You need to politely tell them that this is a subject you prefer not to discuss with them.

When you relate to people in the 90s, you not only need to be sensitive to their feelings but to your own feelings as well. By setting limits in both your business and personal relationships, you set a standard for developing self-respect.

... 4 ...

Good Communicators
Talk to Themselves

Communication involves three things: It reflects how we feel about ourselves, how it affects others, and it is a means by which we are affected by others. Awareness of these three aspects of communication can enhance your ability as a good communicator.

Galen, a Greek philosopher, once said that what goes on in your head and your heart is reflected in your voice. He said it is the voice that mirrors the soul. How right he was. If you feel insecure or suffer from low self-esteem—feeling like you aren't attractive or that you're not a very interesting person—it is usually reflected in your voice quality. Having a nasal voice or a week, inaudible voice, or a gruff, harsh, gravelly voice oftentimes reflects negative feelings you have about yourself. These physical voices that people hear are often the result of inner voices that tell us we are not good enough or that we are unworthy.

We may be good enough but because our inner voices wrongly tell us that we aren't attractive or wonderful, we then tend to speak in unconfident tones and say awful things about ourselves: "Oh, how stupid of me" or "What an idiot I am!" If you find yourself doing that you are using negative "self-talk."

Even though you've had years of negative conditioning, you

can change. You can retrain your inner voice to talk positively—to say encouraging things to yourself and not beat yourself up when you make a mistake. A side benefit to doing this is that oftentimes your vocal tone will improve as you become more confident.

POSITIVE SELF-TALK

One of the most amazing clients I ever had was a successful Texas businessman who told me that every morning after he woke up he would look at himself in the mirror, and in his most positive, enthusiastic voice would say, "Good morning, Wayne. It's so good to see you. We are going to have a terrific day! All kinds of great things are going to happen to us. We are going to have fun and make a lot of money today!" Wayne made millions!

The same thirty-second pep talk won't make you a millionaire—but if you welcome yourself to the world each morning with thirty seconds of positive self-talk, who knows what you may find during the day—more money, new relationships, perhaps a better career!

I have adopted this daily self-talk exercise myself, and can assure you that the good feelings it generates each morning seem to create an aura of positive energy all around me, an energy that touches everyone I come in contact with during the day. I tell many of my patients to take the same thirty seconds in front of the mirror each morning. Just think what you want to happen that day and verbalize it. Say it with all the conviction and reassurance you can muster, and see what happens! It certainly gets your day off to a good start.

KNOW THAT YOU KNOW WHAT YOU KNOW

Besides the negative programming we received as children, another reason we suffer from low self-esteem is that we do not know ourselves. The great Greek philosopher Socrates enlightened the world when he said that the greatest knowledge one can achieve is to "Know Thyself." How true this is!

The key to successful communication is "Know Yourself," or *Know That You Know What You Know*. This includes everything you know and feel about yourself and the world around you, from your innermost introspection to your favorite color to the opinion you have formed from reading newspapers and living life. Of course, this does not mean that you should dominate every conversation with what you know and not let the other person get a word in. It merely means that by knowing what you know you will have a stronger sense of self-confidence that will give you a feeling of security as a communicator, as well as a heightened ability to relate to others.

How well do most of us know ourselves? If you ask yourself, you can probably say immediately what your best friends' favorite colors are, or who their favorite movie stars are, but if you ask yourself the same question about you, it might take some thought before you come up with the answers. It is impossible to like anyone without knowing them. Well, the same is true of yourself. In order to like yourself, you must know yourself.

To help my clients get to know and like themselves better, I ask them to fill out the following *Getting to Know You Survey* (courtesy of G. P. Putnam's Sons, 1987). This simple survey can help you, too. There are no right and wrong answers. Just write down the first answer that comes into your head. You may be surprised at how you see yourself.

GETTING TO KNOW YOU SURVEY

Favorite color _____

Favorite type of music _____

Favorite movies _____

Favorite actors and actresses _____

Biggest turn-ons _____

Biggest turnoffs _____

Favorite books _____

Favorite animal and three adjectives describing it _____

Biggest fantasy _____

Males you admire _____

Females you admire _____

Favorite season _____

Favorite sport _____

Type of clothes you like best _____

Three things you like best _____

Three things you love to do for fun _____

If you were on a desert island, name three people you would want with you _____

If you were on this island, what foods would you want? _____

Favorite place to visit _____

Favorite place to live _____

Favorite car _____

If you could own one luxury item, what would it be? _____

If there was a disaster and you could only take one thing with you, what would it be? _____

My biggest fears are _____

Handsome men make me feel _____

Beautiful women make me feel _____

The two men I love the most are _____

The two women I love the most are _____

What upsets me the most is _____

What makes me laugh is _____

The best thing about me is _____

The worst thing about me is _____

What makes me cry is _____

I could vomit if _____

When I get angry, I _____

Whenever I am attracted to another person, I _____

Whenever I am nervous, I _____

I see myself as _____

Others see me as _____

Next week, I want to _____

Next month, I want to _____

Next year, I want to _____

In the next five years, I want to _____

Create a special place for yourself (a very special place, anywhere you choose). Decorate it. _____
Furnish it. What is outside? What does the inside look like? What does the outside look like? How do you feel in it? What do you do when you are there? Who is there with you? What do you feel like when you are there? _____
_____

I am: (Write down a list of adjectives describing everything you feel you are.) _____
What is the good news about you? _____
What is the bad news about you? _____
What things can you do to get rid of the bad news about you? _____
_____

How many questions in this survey did you have to actually *think* about before you could answer? Did you have to *think* to come up with "The best thing about me is . . ." or "When I get angry, I . . ." or "My favorite color is . . ."? These are things we would certainly know about a best friend, or a relative, but not ourselves, because most of us are not our own best friends!

The next time you feel the impulse to call yourself "stupid" or "ugly," replace that impulse with a healthy program of positive self-talk, the kind of pep talk you would offer a best friend.

SINGING YOUR OWN PRAISES

An extension of positive self-talk is tooting your own horn. One of my clients, an advertising copywriter named Sally, hated tooting her own horn, and all she got for her modesty was the pleasure of watching the other copywriters in her company pass her by on their way up the creative ladder. Was Sally's modesty a virtue? Her boss didn't think so. The truth is, low self-esteem will often masquerade as modesty, and what we really need to do is sing our own praises to the world around us. After all, if we do not show confidence in ourselves, why should anyone else?

There have been literally thousands of books written about

how to improve your self-esteem, but the bottom line is that beyond all the negativity that many of us have had drummed into us by our parents and continue to harbor as adults, most of us feel a lack of self-esteem because there is something missing in our lives.

Building self-esteem can be as simple as filling in what is missing. If you feel inadequate socially because you are uninformed, you can become more informed by reading. If you feel unattractive because you are overweight, happiness may be only a few months of dieting away. If you are unhappy with your job, you can change your job, or your profession! All of these things are within your power! If you don't like something about yourself, change it.

A client of mine, Gail, was a producer's assistant who wanted to move to a job in front of the camera. In school she had trained to be a newscaster, but when she was offered a job as a producer's assistant on a popular talk show, she grabbed it thinking it would eventually lead to on-camera work. Four years later, Gail was still the producer's assistant, typing her boss's letters and wondering what had happened to her ambition. Even if she had the ambition, she wouldn't have been in any shape for on-camera work because she had gained forty pounds out of depression.

Gail was stuck in a frustrating Catch-22—she was depressed because she hated her job, and she couldn't do anything about it because of the weight she had gained from having been so depressed. The good news is that Gail was eventually able to lose the forty pounds she had gained. She did it in three months with a carefully planned diet regimen. Just losing the weight caused her self-esteem to soar, which made her more attractive to others, and with the contacts she had developed as a producer's assistant, and a lot of self-promotion, she was eventually able to get a job as a reporter for a local news station.

Most people are frustrated because they are not allowed to do what they want to do. I see this all of the time in my practice in Hollywood. The most beautiful, brilliant people come to see me—would-be actors, writers, producers, directors—and there is always somebody higher up saying no, no, no to them, often for reasons that have nothing at all to do with their talent.

Is it any wonder that so many people suffer from low self-esteem with all this negative energy in the world? The only way to combat this negative energy is by building *your* own self-esteem from within. Work on your own inner voices. Take some time to get to know yourself and practice *positive self-talk* and know that you know what you know. Taking this advice can make you feel more confident and will reflect how positive you feel about yourself.

... 5 ...

Laugh, Cry, Get Angry,
But Be Anxious for Nothing

The second aspect of communication is our effect on others. How many times have you come away from a conversation or left a party and turned to your mate or your date or your friend, or to yourself, and said, "Did I make a fool of myself?" or "Did they think I was stupid?" or "Did I offend anyone?" Most people do care how they come across to others. In fact, this is why getting up and talking in front of others is the number-one fear. What you say and how you say it can have a profound effect upon others.

It is not always *what* you say—it's not only your tone or the words you use that can affect others. It is whatever comes out of your mouth—even your laugh.

LAUGHING

I was having lunch with a friend at a elegant restaurant in Beverly Hills. We were having a quiet meal when all of a sudden, a woman two tables away broke into a loud, hyena-like laugh. I was struck by the odd image of this elegant woman with this awful shriek of a laugh. The man with her eventually said something else that struck her as funny; once again her laugh pierced the air. She continued to laugh throughout lunch, with absolutely no idea how awful she sounded or how many people she was annoying. Her laughter was so disturbing to everyone that the waiter had to politely ask her to tone it down.

Laughter can be the glitter of communication. It is a wonderful icebreaker, a tension-breaker, good medicine, good exercise, and a means of finding relief in life's misfortunes. We all need to laugh—but when it's appropriate.

A young client of mine, Jane, took a job at an insurance company one summer. She was just eighteen, and it was her first job out of high school. It was also her first exposure to men in the workplace and their flirtations, and they all flirted with sweet, innocent Jane, who, in an attempt to diffuse the situation, developed a nervous giggle, which only encouraged the flirtations all the more and earned her the nickname "the giggler."

A lot of people giggle (often unconsciously) when they are uncomfortable or nervous, when they don't know how to cope with a situation. One day a client, Carla, told me that her son was a drug abuser. The family was doing everything they could to deal with the problem, she said, and she was feeling totally helpless for the first time in her life. What seemed unusual to me was that this woman was laughing after every heart-wrenching detail of her story. Finally I stopped her and asked her why she was giggling as she talked.

"I know it's sad," she answered, "but for some reason I can't help giggling—otherwise I'll cry."

What Carla was doing was giggling in order to hide her embarrassment and her extreme frustration at her inability to cope.

Actually, Carla's is a very common reaction. Whenever we are overwhelmed by emotion, there can be the urge to laugh. This is why some people laugh at funerals.

Sometimes the urge to laugh inappropriately can be overpowering. One of my clients, Judy, was friends with an amateur opera singer, Dorie, who loved to throw dinner parties. After dinner, Dorie would invite everybody into the living room to listen to her sing the worst opera, with her husband accompanying her on the piano. Listening to Dorie sing was like pulling a cat's tail and hearing it scream. That was exactly the image that went running through Judy's mind as she sat in the living room listening to Dorie sing. It was all she could do to contain herself.

"I imagined the cat hitting the same note as Dorie," Judy told me. "I became absolutely hysterical. All I could do was put my hand to my mouth like I had to sneeze. Eventually I ran out of the room and pretended I was sick only to become convulsive with laughter." As a result, Judy will never go to one of Dorie's dinner parties because she knows she can't control her laughter.

If you find yourself in a similar situation, you can handle it the way Judy did, by covering your face with your handkerchief and leaving the room.

If, on the other hand, you are a "giggler," a simple breathing exercise can help you gain control over the urge to giggle. If you find yourself giggling at an inappropriate moment, or just smiling inappropriately, take a breath in, hold it for a few seconds, and let your breath out slowly and simply.

Inappropriate laughter, whether it is unintentional or intentional, can have a devastating effect on others. It is in all our best interests to get to know the sound of our laughter, and to listen *when* we laugh. Do you laugh in appropriate situations? Do you laugh at other people's misfortunes or embarrassment? Do you laugh to cover your own nervousness? If you do, then you need to re-evaluate your laugh habits, because inappropriate laughter can be a real turnoff.

Many people who see me professionally ask, "Dr. Glass, can I change my laugh?" "Of course you can change your laugh," I tell them, and many do.

The first thing you need to do is listen to your laugh. If you have a very loud, guffawing laugh and you want to temper it, try laughing through your nose instead of your mouth and keeping your mouth closed. Your laughing may be even easier to control than you think. Unless you are really disturbed by your laugh and want to change it, I don't ordinarily encourage people to change the way they laugh because laughter that comes from the heart can be music to the ears.

CRYING

Major corporate executives have come into my office and vented their frustrations through tears. One actor burst into tears one day because he felt horrible about how his latest movie had turned out. He had been proud of his performance, but the director and the editor had ruined the film in the editing room. He cried because he had no control over the situation.

As adults, we should never be ashamed of crying, of letting out our emotions. Our only concern should be that when we do cry, we do it in a safe, appropriate situation, which unfortunately isn't always possible.

For example, if you cry at work, where bursting into tears can hurt you, try to bite your lip, slap yourself, or pinch yourself until you find a safe place to let your tears go—the bathroom, the car, or wherever. A newscaster friend of mine was reporting a story one day about a six-year-old child who had been killed in a very brutal way. It took all the self-control he could muster to keep the tears from welling up and overflowing right on the air. As soon as they went to commercial, he broke down. Being the professional he was, he managed to hold himself together while he was on camera, and being the man he was, he was able to let himself cry when it was safe to do so.

Crying in the workplace, however, can be dangerous. One of my clients, Randi, was being yelled at one day by her boss for not making enough sales. Instead of saying, "You have no right to yell at me like this," Randi started to cry. From that time on, her psychologically unbalanced boss tormented her and tried to make her cry whenever he could.

Unfortunately, people derive a feeling of power from being able to make other people cry. If you find yourself in a situation similar to Randi's, do whatever you can to protect yourself. If you are completely overwhelmed and do not feel equipped to put your foot down and say, "Look, stop yelling at me! This is not acceptable," leave the room, and then do what you have to do to see that this person does not abuse you in the future. It may even be in your best interest to find another job.

On the other hand, crying can be the most effective way of expressing yourself. I will never forget the night of the Academy Awards presentation in 1988 when Academy–Award winning actress Marlee Matlin, deaf since birth, spoke publicly for the very first time. There literally wasn't a dry eye in the auditorium. Her words, her perfect diction, and sensuous tones tugged at the heartstrings of the most famous celebrities as millions of viewers throughout the world, including myself, cried.

We all need to feel more free to cry—to release tears. Crying may even bond you to others. One of my clients, Barbara, never felt close to her husband, until one day he cried in her arms as he openly expressed the frustration of their relationship. For the first time, she said, "I felt close to him because he finally let his emotions show." She felt totally open with him, which, incidentally, saved her marriage.

Crying can even bond you closer to yourself. It puts you in touch with your own feelings and, in doing so, enables you to communicate with others on a more intimate level. Medically, crying has been found to release a chemical through tears that helps to reduce stress. Crying is not a sign of weakness; on the contrary, it takes a strong person to face their emotions and let them out. In fact, not facing your emotions and expressing them can actually weaken you. So it's no wonder that those people who don't cry to express their sadness or frustration die each year of heart attacks and other stress-induced illnesses.

Crying, in essence, releases the volcano that churns inside all of us. So don't hold back when you need to cry—just make sure you do it in a safe place around safe people.

COPING WITH ANXIETY

Unlike laughter, which breaks down walls and opens up communication between people, anxiety, which is just as contagious, creates walls and keeps us from communicating with one another.

Tanya, a producer client of mine, hired a friend of hers, Bob, who she thought was bright and articulate, and who she thought was a good writer for a script for her movie. They spent hours going through the script, with Tanya putting in all of her points of view. She was excited to work with Bob because she felt that through her interviews he captured what she wanted expressed in the film. When she took a look at the draft of this script it was another story. She was appalled that he missed the entire point, put in too many of his own ideas that had nothing to do with what they discussed, and had limited writing abilities. Because they were friends and because they were bound by a contract, she wanted to make this work; however, her anxiety about the project stood in the way of their communicating with one another. She was so angry at what had happened that she was short-tempered and verbally insulting to Bob. Bob, in turn, was devastated and felt as though he couldn't continue working with Tanya under the conditions. Until Tanya was able to let go of her anxiety by expressing to Bob all her concerns so that Bob could in turn rectify the problems, their working relationship could not continue. These two anxiety-ridden people were finally able to diffuse their short fuses through honest, calm, rational, open *communication*.

Research has shown that all of us get anxieties from time to time. We're anxious about a number of things like not having an emotionally satisfying relationship, and the fear of missing out on the rewards of a lasting relationship like family and children.

Many of us are anxious about being lonely. Even though we may not be alone, we can still feel lonely.

Many people are anxious about their health, fueled by the epidemics of cancer, heart disease, and now AIDS. More than ever, people are concerned about what they are eating and how their diet is affecting their health, their blood sugar, their cholesterol level, and their future lives.

We are anxious about our physical appearance. This is particularly true here in Hollywood where I live and work, where a person simply *has* to be a certain weight and *have* a certain look or physical appearance.

Finally, there are job-related anxieties. Are we really doing what we want to do? Are we being paid as we deserve to be? Will we have our job next week?

In my years as a speech therapist and communications specialist treating the most profoundly handicapped to the biggest stars in Hollywood, I have learned one thing for certain: *We all have anxieties*. When we are manifesting these anxieties outwardly, other people feel anxious around us.

The good news is that you can combat anxiety through openly expressing how you feel, handling the problems that come your way, and breathing out your anxieties.

When you get anxious, you take more shallow breaths and you do not release air as frequently as you do when you are not anxious. As a result, you get a buildup of carbon dioxide, which gives some people very severe headaches, others shortness of breath, and others a faster heartbeat. In order for your body to function normally, you have to breathe oxygen in and release carbon dioxide. In order to release the tension you need to oxygenate yourself.

Relaxation breathing techniques have been around since the teaching of the ancient yogis in India, and the object of the relaxation breathing technique is to achieve good breath control and calm you down. You can do this exercise any time of the day or night. It's very simple. You need to do these exercises gently and slowly so you don't hyperventilate. First, lie down on your back on a flat surface and place one hand on your upper chest and the other on your abdomen. Make sure only your abdomen moves when you are breathing—not your chest. Then slowly and gently breathe in through the mouth for three seconds, filling your abdomen with air. Hold your breath for three seconds, and then gently and slowly exhale through the mouth for six seconds. You will feel your abdominal muscles contracting as you let all the air out through your mouth. Do this about ten times.

Next, sit up, with your head up and shoulders, spine, and back straight. Place one hand on your upper chest and the other on your abdomen. Make sure you keep your upper chest from moving and just move your abdominal muscles.

Next, gently and slowly take a breath in through the mouth for three seconds. Be sure to push your abdomen *out* as you fill up with air. Then, hold the breath for three seconds. Now, slowly and gently exhale through your mouth for six seconds. You can do this in your car or at work—anywhere.

Another exercise to help you really get tension and anxiety out is the Tension Blow-Out exercise. This exercise will help you release your immediate anxiety or anger by allowing you to oxygenate yourself and expel the negative feelings building up inside you. This technique can also be used when you burst out laughing inappropriately due to tension. The Tension Blow-Out will help you regain your composure by allowing you to coordinate your breathing with talking, and holding in the air for a moment allows you the split second to decide whether you should let the other person have it or let the anger die out with your breath-flow. I've taught this technique to prisoners and received letters back from the prison warden saying, "Now instead of the prisoners beating up each other, they're breathing on each other."

In the Tension Blow-Out exercise you do the same thing you did in the relaxation breathing exercise by taking in the air through the mouth and holding it for three seconds. However, now blow out the air until you have no air left. Keep pushing until you are completely out of air.

Do not breathe for three seconds. Now immediately do this three times. On the fourth time you can proceed to breathe normally. You may feel a little light-headed—don't worry about it as it will go away. You should feel much better and less angry since this exercise helps to oxygenate you. If you are still angry, repeat this exercise until you don't feel anxious or angry.

Another way you can get rid of pent-up anxiety is by *defusing* it. A clothing-designer friend of mine, Marva, was very anxious about a job interview with a company that she had wanted to join for several years. On the day of the interview she felt her anxiety building from the moment she woke up, and by the time she arrived at the interview she was on the verge of an anxiety attack. She was afraid she was not going to be able to make it through the interview.

Instead of trying to conceal her anxiety, the first thing Marva did when she sat down opposite the lady conducting the interview was to say, "I'm feeling very anxious right now." That simple statement defused her anxiety and enabled Marva not only to make it through the interview, but to get the job as well.

The bottom line is that we all harbor anxieties, which can build at the most inappropriate time. What we need to do is simply "go with the flow"—the *flow of breath*. Just take in that breath and flow it out. It may seem trivial, but this flow is the basis of helping to control an anxiety-free life.

DEALING WITH YOUR ANGER

The basic reason we become angry is because we feel that we are not treated with the respect we deserve. When we feel we are being taken for granted, used, or we are frustrated, we become angry. Always confront your anger immediately and do not hold it in. Otherwise it can escalate and get out of hand just like it did with Kimberly and Linda.

Kimberly and Linda were best friends who had a lot in common. One day, Kimberly, knowing how much Linda liked amethysts, gave her an amethyst necklace that she had bought for herself two years earlier and never had worn, but she never thought she would see the necklace on Linda's mother.

The loan of the necklace had been just that—a loan. Linda's mother had seen it one day, admired it, and Linda had lent it to her for the evening, not thinking that Kimberly would take offense at seeing the necklace around her mother's neck. It turned out Kimberly was offended, but didn't say anything. Kimberly began to notice other things about Linda that turned her off—but she didn't say anything to Linda. Finally, one day when Linda cancelled out on their vacation plans because of an unexpected job prospect, Kimberly blew up at her for it and even brought up the "necklace" incident along with Linda's other "faults." Linda was stunned. She couldn't understand why Kimberly didn't bring up these things at the time they happened.

The result was that Linda lost complete trust in Kimberly. Eventually the relationship ended. Kimberly seemed sweet, but underneath she was angry and kept score instead of confronting her friend directly and honestly about things that bothered her.

The lesson is a simple one—don't keep lists. If you have anger inside you, let it out. Tell the other person what's bothering you at the time it happens; otherwise the anger inside you will grow until it poisons you, the other person, or both of you. If you have to raise your voice, shout, or scream—do it. Just be sure to release it. The silent treatment doesn't work. All it does is serve to alienate people and close off the lines of communication.

Sometimes when you are angry you may say or do something you'll regret. So before you do so—do the "Tension Blow-Outs," where you take a breath of air in—hold it and blow it out—repeating the procedure three times, releasing all your anger when you exhale each breath. Doing them can help you release your anger immediately. Next, *calmly confront* the person who angered you. Never become involved in violence. There is no place for violence in communication. If you ever feel you want to choke someone, leave the room, or the building, or the state, if necessary—long enough to "blow out," "yell out," or defuse your anger.

... 6 ...

You're Known Not for How You Act, But How You React

You can see the importance of how your communication affects your self-esteem, and how your communication affects others— whether it is how you laugh, cry, express your anxieties, or express your anger. The way others' communication affects you is the third area you need to examine in order to understand what good communication is all about.

REJECTION

We've all gotten rejected at one point or another in our lives, and being rejected is definitely an instance where someone else's communication can affect the outcome of your life. I see people in my practice—actors—who are constantly dealing with rejection, which unfortunately is the nature of the entertainment business, where *No* is heard far more often than *Yes*. Constantly hearing *No, No, No* unfortunately can do a lot of damage to a person's self-esteem. A lot of people deal with rejection by trying to ignore it, saying instead, "The timing wasn't right," or offer other rational excuses. No matter how well you take it— rejection still hurts, it still feels bad, and nobody likes it.

One of my actress clients was getting plenty of auditions but she was not getting any actual jobs. On her agent's advice, she started wearing flat shoes because he felt she might be "too tall," but she was still not getting any jobs. Finally, I suggested Diana have her agent call the casting agents and ask why she was not getting any roles. A few days later, he called and told her they thought she wasn't tall enough. "They thought I wasn't tall enough?" she repeated, "you thought I was too tall."

"I know," he said, "but they're doing the hiring, and they say you're not tall enough."

So Diana started auditioning in heels, and then, of course, there were those who thought she was too tall.

Sometimes you are rejected because you just don't fit what the person is looking for. It may have very little to do with you at all—as in Diana's case. Her rejection is a natural part of her business.

If you are constantly being rejected by people socially, it may be time to strip yourself naked, so to speak, and examine the way you relate to other people.

One of the unhappiest clients I ever treated was a woman named Betty who had little bitty teeth, a very tight jaw, closed mouth, a very pinched squint, and a non-giving, closed personality. Her husband was a successful businessman and they did some socializing, but only with her husband's business associates. They took the associates out to dinner, but the associates would never reciprocate. Their wives felt very uncomfortable around Betty and they consistently rejected her invitations to have lunch with her.

The first thing I noticed about Betty when I met her was her smile and her little bitty teeth. I sent her to Dr. Henry Yamada, a dentist in Los Angeles who specializes in cosmetic dentistry. Through bonding, he made her teeth appear larger. Now when she smiled you could see her teeth, and she actually became very pretty. We then developed an exercise to stop Betty from squinting, which enabled her to open her eyes so that her face was no longer so "pinched." When she became nervous, she learned to breathe her way through situations instead of squinting her way through them. She also started reading the newspaper and became more aware of the world around her, and she began asking questions of other people to draw them out rather than indulging in her own self-consciousness.

Betty was able to turn the rejection she was experiencing into something positive by becoming a person who was not only more physically attractive, but more attractive and confident both inside and out. Unfortunately, many people refuse to learn from rejection. Sometimes you just have to take that pained look at yourself and ask yourself why you are being rejected. What you see can truly be eye-opening and life-opening!

Often the rejection we feel coming from others is actually us rejecting ourselves. It may sound crazy but too frequently this is just the case! If you feel unattractive and you broadcast this feeling through poor attitude, poor posture, and poor facial expression, other people will see what you project and react accordingly. If you go to a party rejecting yourself, others will usually reject you, too.

It's difficult to get through life without having been rejected. After all, the most successful businessmen and women, the most famous actors and actresses in Hollywood—all of them have more than their share of rejection, particularly because these people are risk takers.

Several years ago, Melanie Griffith came to me in tears because she had been constantly rejected in auditions, for role after role. The directors did not like the sound of her voice. Instead of giving up, she fought the rejection. She came to me and worked on her voice, and the result was an Academy-Award nomination for *Working Girl!*

Although none of us want rejection in our lives, the good part about it is that if you are willing to learn from it—find out *why* you were rejected and then do something constructive about it—a lot of personal growth will come out of it. If it is unjustified rejection, there is growth in realizing that it is unjustified and that it has nothing to do with us and then rising above it. We need to look at our rejection as less of a threat and more as a growth opportunity. Sure, it hurts, there is no question about it, but you can use rejection to turn yourself into a winner. The key to being a winner is finding out which rock has the gold nugget underneath it, and by surrounding yourself with as many loving, caring, supportive people as you can.

TOXIC COMMUNICATORS

I recently conducted a survey, asking people what makes them unhappy the most. Aside from financial and health issues, the majority of people said that their number-one problem was dealing with difficult people in their lives.

In spending thousands of hours talking to clients, I've heard story after story about that one difficult person who was making their life miserable. Even though the names and circumstances are all different, the story is the same.

Dr. Susan Forward wrote an excellent book called *Toxic Parents* and how you even have to eliminate toxic family members from your life. Taking this one step further, I would say that there are also "toxic people" poisoning our lives, people who are not life supporting or who are not happy to see us grow and succeed. These people do everything they can to sabotage our efforts to lead happy, productive lives. *THESE PEOPLE SHOULD BE CUT OUT OF YOUR LIFE!*

Once, I was giving a seminar in Sacramento to a group of government officials, and at one point I said, "If there are people in your lives who do not support you, who do not treat you with the respect and dignity you deserve, get them out of your life—don't allow them into any part of your daily life." After the seminar was over, a very tall, handsome gentleman came up to me with tears in his eyes. "Dr. Glass," he said, "how can you say that you must just let these people go from your life? What about the friends I've had for twenty or thirty years? What about sentimentality? Doesn't that count for anything?" Although I was sensitive to his concerns, I told him, "There is no sentimentality when somebody is abusing you, dragging you down, and not letting you be the best you can be. Sentimentality is for sweetness, for lovingness, for people who are positive forces in your life, who have always treated you with kindness and dignity and respect. It has nothing to do with people who sabotage you and who don't allow you to grow."

The gentleman finally admitted that when he heard my comments, he kept thinking of his wife of twenty years and how he knew what I said was right and that he needed to get out of his "toxic" marriage. Being honest with yourself after years of self-deception can be a very scary experience, but it is a necessary step to take.

Having heard thousands of stories in my own private practice, I have sorted the most common types of toxic people into five major categories—The Five Toxic Communication Styles—which I will share with you. You may know some more yourself, but here are some recognizable types of toxic communicators:

1. **The instigator** is a person who communicates by trying to make trouble for other people. It may be that their lives are so miserable and so dull that the only way to generate some excitement is by verbally stirring up the waters in other people's lives. They often communicate by innuendo—"Oh, I'm sure Frank is completely devoted to you, even though he spent the afternoon with Debby the other day" or "I'm not one to pry, but isn't Robert supposed to be working exclusively for you? I saw him doing some work for Jane."

Set the instigator straight immediately. Remind them they are only responsible for their own business. Directness works best with them. Use phrases like "Are you saying this to upset me?" or "Are you trying to instigate a problem here?" Put the ball back in their lap. In essence, embarrass them and let them know you are aware of the game they are playing. If you do confront them, they will often develop a newfound respect for you.

2. **The accuser**'s toxic communication style reflects their own self-hate, insecurity, and defensiveness.

Here is an example of the communication of toxic accusers I overheard at the table next to me while I was having dinner one evening:

"You were the reason we were late," he said.

"No, it was you," she said.

"It was you and your makeup," he said.

"It was you and your phone calls," she said.

"Look, you're always late. Everyone in your family is always late. They never taught you to how to be on time."

If you are being verbally attacked by an accuser, let them know after the first accusation that you will not tolerate being verbally abused. Let them know that there is no reason for them to attack or accuse you and that they can have better interaction with you if they ask questions of you and then listen for the answers instead of accusing you.

For example, here's how a toxic accuser's conversation could be defused:

"You were the reason we were late," he said.

"How did you come to that conclusion?" she said.

"Well, it takes you forever to put on your makeup," he said.

"Honey, don't you think that the last three phone calls you made right before we left contributed to our being late?" she said.

"You're right. I guess we're both guilty," he said.

Asking questions, not making a counter-accusation, and using a term of endearment such as "honey" and the word "our" instead of "your," clearly changes an accuser's response to a more positive one.

3. **The meddler** loves to give advice. Often, meddlers don't have the experience or the professional expertise to match their advice and they frequently live their lives vicariously through others. Janet and Mark had quite a nice relationship that worked for them until Stella began coaching Janet on what she should or shouldn't accept from Mark. Stella's interference almost cost Janet her relationship with Mark. When Mark confronted her and said, "Look, this doesn't sound like you. Who has been filling your head with these fallacies?" Janet admitted it was Stella, and immediately called Stella and told her to stay out of her relationship with Mark. You need to set the meddler straight immediately and tell them to butt out.

4. **The cut-you-downer** is the kind of communicator who, when you receive a raise, will comment on how good the company is about giving "automatic" raises as employee incentives. If you lose weight, the cut-you-downer will comment, "You shouldn't lose too much weight or you will get sick." Nothing is ever good enough for the cut-you-downer. They will find the cloud in any silver lining. In essence, they are unhappy with themselves so they try to make you miser-

able so they can better relate to you. Like the other toxic communicators, you need to immediately confront the cut-you-downer and let them know that you will not tolerate their negative comments and their insistence upon looking for the bad in everything positive you share with them.

5. **The back-stabber** is the person who works best behind your back, telling harmful secrets about you, sabotaging you. They masquerade as smiling friends, but in reality are the worst of enemies. They are spies looking for information to destroy you with.

The best way to protect yourself from a back-stabber is to see them do their work to someone else and catch yourself when you start to think, "They would never do that to me." If they did it to someone else, you can be sure that you are next. These people are the most toxic and need to be cut out of your life forever. With friends like these, you certainly don't need enemies.

If you can see any people you know in any of these categories, and you find that you *cannot* communicate with them no matter how hard you try, you may want to remove yourself from their presence.

The key to dealing with these toxic communicators is to recognize before whom you stand so that you can confront them honestly and openly. If you can't get through to them—keep your distance.

If you find yourself exhibiting any of these toxic-communication patterns, stop it immediately. Perhaps it's the reason you may be having difficulty "winfluencing" people. There is no excuse for this type of behavior, so eliminate these toxic-communication patterns once and for all.

... 7 ...

Positive Criticism

If you care about another person's welfare and you can see that what they are doing is very damaging to them, it is important to offer your critical opinion. In this case, it is not "what you say" but "how you say it." There are certain "buzz" words and phrases that you need to use in order not to hurt the other person's feelings and allow them to save face. The key buzz words and phrases are:

- "It may be in your best interest . . ."
- "You may want to consider . . ."
- "May I suggest something to you? . . ."
- "I would never do anything to hurt your feelings, but I want to offer my opinion, if I can . . ."
- "I'm on your side, so don't take what I'm about to say as critical . . ."
- "I want you to know that I have your best interest at heart . . ."
- "Please don't feel offended, but it's important that we put our egos into our back pockets and look at what happened objectively . . ."

The key in giving criticism is to offer a solution that will show the person that you care about them and support them. You don't want to say, "You dumbbell, how could you do that?" or "I can't believe you did anything that stupid!" If you do, you run the risk of putting the other person on the defensive, and making it difficult or impossible for them to listen to you and process what you have to offer.

Most of the time, people don't want to hear your criticism unless they ask you for it, and even then they still may not want to hear it. However, if you couch it in endearing, positive terms, they will definitely hear what you have to say. Recently, I saw one of my clients on a television talk show. He was awful—sloppy, inappropriate, acting like he was on drugs and not making any sense.

Knowing that he was my client, a number of people called me to tell me how terrible he was and how he was ruining his career by coming across like that. They noticed that even the host was uncomfortable with him. After all the work that he had done in terms of his camera presence and speaking skills, I was very disappointed and angry with him. However, I knew that he would never hear what I had to say if I didn't approach the problem with love and sensitivity. Here is how our conversation went when he came in to see me.

"How did you feel about your performance last night?"

"Fine," he answered cavalierly.

"I want you to know that since I met you I have always been in your corner, and I completely believe in your talent and in your abilities. So I would like to offer you some suggestions about last night."

"Go ahead," he said, listening quietly.

"Your performance last night was not one of the best situations I have seen you in. It's really important for you to sit up straight, look at your host, and only react to questions he asks you. If you are not happy with the way the interview is going, don't get angry on television—just redirect the subject matter. You also need to remember to breathe and to control your nervousness."

My client listened attentively and appreciated my input. He then wanted to practice being videotaped in an interview situation. Had I not couched my criticism with terms of endearment and my support of him, he would have become defensive and possibly even walked out. I also offered him alternatives— how to make the performance look better. I didn't leave him dangling there, telling him, "You did a terrible job. Don't ever do it again." I didn't chastise him—I supported him.

Couching your criticism with the "buzz" words and phrases mentioned above and offering an alternative to the situation you are criticizing is positive, constructive criticism.

DEALING WITH CRITICAL PEOPLE

There are friends who are so critical that you always feel on guard when you are around them. These people are full of negative "buzz" words like "could have" and "should have," and they are always ready to offer their negative view of everything you say and do, and everything that comes your way in life.

The only way to deal with these "friends"—if you want to keep them in your life—is to break them of their negativity, or simply get them out of your life because they can be dangerous to your self-esteem.

A friend is not someone who tells you how to live your life. A true friend is not a source of "negative" criticism. For example, Edith and Margaret both considered themselves to be Christians. Edith tried to live her life in a Christian manner, but did not go to church regularly nor read the Bible daily nor pray in tongues as her friend Margaret did. Margaret would constantly criticize Edith and tell her that she was not being a very good Christian because she did not practice her Christianity in the same way that Margaret did. This was a constant source of frustration in their relationship. Edith finally told Margaret that she considered herself to be a good Christian and told Margaret to mind her own business or find another friend.

Margaret was shocked at Edith's ultimatum. "After all," she said, "I was just trying to help you." Edith then replied that she appreciated her help, but she needed to stop criticizing her and making her feel like an inferior being for having a different point of view. Nobody has the right to tell another person how to pray, how to live their life, or how to exist, without the other person asking for the advice. When asked for advice, you must couch what you say in loving, non-critical terms.

We're all aware of the stereotype of the nagging housewife who perpetually criticizes her husband for leaving his socks around, for not taking out the garbage, for forgetting to do an errand. Instead of constantly berating her man, she'll get better results if instead of saying, "You always leave your clothes lying around," she says, "Honey, I know you're in a hurry, but please don't leave your clothes in the middle of the room because then I have more work to do."

Tone of voice is extremely important as well. You need to eliminate the hostile edge to your voice and say what you have to say with love and kindness in order to achieve optimal results and to be heard.

HOW TO BENEFIT FROM A CRITIC

Criticism is usually one person's opinion, and because it is only "opinion," it can often be the source of wrong information. For example, look at the opinions of the television critics like Siskel and Ebert or Gary Franklin or Rex Reed. Most of the time I disagree with what these people have to say about the movies I've seen. In fact, they rarely even agree with one another! All of what these critics say is nothing other than "opinion."

If any of these critics were former film producers or directors many of us would consider their opinions in a different light. Their opinions would mean more because they would be making their judgments based on more objective criteria. If they would say more about how they would improve the movie instead of just tearing it down with their "twenty-twenty hindsight," more people would be more respectful of their points of view.

For example, if you go to a doctor who is a specialist rather than a general practitioner, he can offer you a more valid opinion based on his expertise. If you have a skin problem, the opinion of your dermatologist may be more valuable than the opinion of your general practitioner. The same is true in my field. If a family member criticizes your speech, you may not take it as seriously as the opinion of a trained communications specialist or speech pathologist.

The main problem with criticism is that people tell you what the problem is, but nobody gives you any alternatives. My philosophy is that if you are going to criticize someone, you must give them alternatives along with the criticism. That is why getting criticism from a professional whose background you respect and who can offer alternatives is valuable.

If you respect the person, their criticism may have a lot of merit and you may learn from it, but if somebody gives you improper or inaccurate criticism, you may want to stop them immediately.

This happened to one of my clients, a multi-talented performer, who encountered a habitually negative manager who felt that it was his job in life to criticize everybody who walked into his office. Unfortunately, he used his position to take his own insecurities and hostilities out on people. The manager questioned my multi-talented client about her career goals, and she told him that she would like to do it all—singing, acting, dancing, and writing. The manager replied, "You're a mess. You're all over the place." My client looked directly at him and confidently said, "I am not all over the place. I have a lot of talent in a lot of areas. If you are not able to manage me in all of those areas, I don't think we have anything else to talk about."

Nobody had ever confronted the manager like that before, which, by the way, impressed him, and he became very eager to sign my client. Unfortunately, she was not impressed with him and sought representation elsewhere.

In this particular case, the criticism was not merited. When one encounters this kind of unwarranted negative criticism, one has three choices: One can either laugh it off, confront it, or just leave the criticism and the critical person behind.

On the other hand, there are times when people will offer you good, sound, constructive critical advice. On these occasions, you want to do several things. First, you want to let the other person know that their criticism is important to you—it is valued. You may want to say, "I really appreciate your criticism. Your opinion means a lot to me."

Secondly, you want to get the most out of your valued critic by asking them to explain in greater detail—elaborate—what you need to do, in their opinion, to improve yourself in order to be the best you can be.

BEING YOUR OWN BEST CRITIC

One thing my most successful clients have in common is their ability to be their own best critics. They have the ability to step back and analyze themselves, their performances, and different aspects of their lives.

I had the privilege of working with Julio Iglesias on his hit song "To All the Girls," and I was so impressed with his ability to dissect what was right and what was wrong in his singing when recording his song. He is a great self-critic, and that is why he is the world's most popular singing star. If his pronunciation or phrasing was off, or if his singing was not up to par, he would be the first to take note and he would go back and redo the track. At the same time, he does not take himself too seriously. He projects humility with a sense of humor with comments like, "I don't know why these people think I'm sexy . . . I'm just an average guy from Spain with skinny bird legs singing songs." Tom Jones is another performer who doesn't take himself so seriously on-stage. I recently watched him perform and was amazed by how he was able to laugh at and criticize himself, which I found endearing.

When one looks at oneself in an objective, positive, critical manner, one begins to grow. The "Self-Critic Test" that I have devised (p. 97) involves five aspects of your life that should be listed in a right-hand column: (1) your social life; (2) your work life; (3) your professional life; (4) your family life; and (5) your body and physical status.

On the top of the page draw and list (1) what is the present situation; (2) what would be the ideal situation; and (3) what steps do I need to take to make the ideal come true. You need to draw three columns for each of the five categories. In the first column under social life, for example, you need to ask yourself what your present social life is like right now. Do you have a lot of friends or not? How often do you socialize? How often do you meet new people?

Under your work life, you need to write down what is going on at your present job. Do you have the job you want? Are you paying your bills? Are you making enough money to make ends meet? In the third category, under your professional life, you need to ask yourself what is the present status of your career? Are you accomplishing your career dreams? In the fourth category, your family life, you need to ask yourself what is the present status of the relationship with the people close to you—your children, your parents, relatives, your boyfriend or girlfriend, your husband, your wife. In the fifth category, your body and physical status, you need to ask yourself what is the current status of your physical appearance. Go down the list, from your hair to your face to your body to your clothes to your weight to your speech. Evaluate yourself honestly. Who are you inside and what do you look like outside? Describe yourself objectively and honestly.

In the second column, write what you would like your *ideal* social life, work life, professional life, family life, and physical appearance to be. If there was a fairy godmother who could give you whatever you want, write what you'd really like her to give you in each of these five areas.

Finally, in the third column, list all of the steps you would take in order to accomplish all of your fantasies that you described in the second column.

Let's take, for example, the social life category, where your present situation is that you have few friends, no romance, and you don't spend much time going out socializing. In the second column your ideal situation may be to have a special person in your life, to go to different parties, and to literally have your dance card filled with activities on the weekend. In the third column you actually list the steps you need to take to improve your social life. For example, you might join a dating service, you might take tennis lessons, you might have friends come over and invite their friends to your home for dinners.

This self-critic test is a great way to look at yourself objectively, evaluate your life, and make the necessary changes to have a happy, fulfilled life. By simply taking a look at yourself realistically and deciding what you can do about different areas in your life to change them, you can become your own best critic in a very "positive" way.

It is important to note that being your own best critic does not mean "beating" yourself up. It does not mean putting out negative PR about yourself or tearing yourself down. Beating yourself up and negative PR is contagious. If you constantly tell people how fat you are and how you are constantly trying to diet, it won't be long before others will take over and start telling you how fat you are and helping you to stay on your diet by monitoring everything that goes in your mouth.

EXAMPLE OF SELF-CRITIC TEST

	Present Situation	*Ideal Situation*	*Steps I Need to Take to Make the Ideal Come True*
1. SOCIAL LIFE	No romance. Few friends. No parties. Can't meet. right person. Dull weekends.	To have a special person in my life. To go to parties weekly. To have a lot of activities on the weekend.	Join a dating service. Get friends to fix me up. Be more open. Take more risks. Give dinner parties. Join gym. Smile and be friendly.

(You fill in the rest.)

2. WORK LIFE

3. PROFESSIONAL LIFE

4. FAMILY LIFE

5. BODY AND PHYSICAL STATUS

LISTENING TO POSITIVE CRITICISM

No matter if the criticism is negative or positive, criticism of any kind makes most of us feel uncomfortable, vulnerable, and even rejected. There are two crucial things to consider when you listen to criticisms. Number one, who is the source, and two, do they have your best interest at heart. In answering these two questions, you can determine if the criticism is negative or positive.

If you find yourself constantly being criticized so that you can't feel comfortable being yourself, the criticism is negative. If the person criticizing you is criticizing you because of how your actions affect them and their opinions of you, you may not want to have this negative criticizer involved in your life.

One of my clients, Marilyn, was involved with a negative criticizer and could do no right. One time she and Bob—her boyfriend—went out to dinner on the docked ship, the *Queen Mary*, and they had to wait in line before being seated. Marilyn proceeded to rock back and forth as they were standing in line. She teasingly said to Bob, "Let's see if we can rock the boat." Now it's obvious that one can't rock the *Queen Mary*, but Marilyn was just being funny and cute. Her smile quickly turned to a frown when Bob said in a suppressive, whispered tone, "Stop drawing attention to yourself and sit down." He literally took the wind out of Marilyn's sails and eventually the wind out of the relationship. The last straw came when, at the dinner table, Marilyn noticed a couple who ordered a crawfish dinner with the eyes, claws, and tentacles still intact. Marilyn, feeling playful, pointed and said, "Look at that! Doesn't that look scary!" Bob once again hushed her, and lightly slapping her hand, said, "Stop pointing. You're embarrassing me."

Throughout the relationship, he continued to inhibit Marilyn until she no longer was able to be her warm, spontaneous self. The result of this negative criticism ended the relationship.

Similarly, Janet and Gail's relationship died due to negative criticism. These close college friends hadn't seen each other in years. When they finally got together, all Janet seemed to do was criticize Gail and her beliefs. All Gail heard from Janet was, "You should eat this . . . You should wear this . . . You should buy this . . ." It seemed as though everything she did got on Janet's nerves. After letting Janet know how she felt, she lost respect for Janet and didn't want such a negatively critical person in her life anymore, and found that she felt a major relief in letting go of this critical friend from her past.

Negative critics like Bob or Janet will often disguise themselves as friends and say "I'm telling you this for your own good" or "because I care." In reality they only care about how your actions affect them or make them look or how they can control your behavior. With negative criticizers, you have to consider the source. These criticizers are usually very suppressive individuals who do not have your best interest at heart.

There is a way to criticize someone that allows the person being criticized to "save face" and to help that person become "all they can be." This is called positive criticism and should be welcomed.

Most of us aren't familiar with positive criticism and our initial reaction to positive criticizers might be "Who do you think you are?" or "What do you know?" or "You're just saying that because you're jealous." However, after you've considered the source, and have had some time to "lick your wounds" and recover from the initial shock, you will see that the criticism is in your best interest. If you take heed and follow the advice you will often become a better person because of it.

If you consider the source and realize that they may have your best interest at heart, you will be able to benefit tremendously. A client of mine who was a successful lecturer wanted to be a television reporter. She went to the best agent in town who told her that if she wanted to do that she'd have to lose forty pounds. She held in her anger and when she left his office she called me, crying and cursing this agent. After she finished I asked her if she could try to put her ego in her back pocket and really listen to the criticism, which may have been designed to help her. First, I told her that this agent was the best agent in the country and really knew what he was talking about in the television industry. In essence, I was helping her to consider the source. Second, I helped her see that the agent had her best interest at heart. If she looked good, she would be hired and if she was hired, she would be doing what she wanted to do, and both she *and* the agent would benefit. Two months later, she succeeded in losing the weight and now is regularly seen on television.

Positive criticism can be the best gift you will ever receive if you use it to your advantage. If you take heed and realize that the person who is offering you the criticism has honorable motives and is on your side, you can eventually end up having a more fulfilling, complete life.

GIVING ADVICE

Most of us have been asked "Do you want me to give you some free advice?" Well, it may not cost the person getting the advice anything, but if you are the person offering the advice, you may wind up paying dearly for the privilege of giving it.

Consider Clara and Rita, who had met in college and had continued to be friends after they graduated and got jobs. One day Clara had a fight with her boyfriend, Roger, and she could not bring herself to call him. So she called Rita, asking for her advice.

Clara had never asked Rita for advice before, since Clara was by far the more experienced in relationships and was usually the one who gave advice. But Rita offered the best advice she could as she tried to be fair to both Clara and Roger. The advice was definitely not what Clara wanted to hear and she lashed out at Rita by saying "Why am I even asking you? You've never had a decent relationship in your life!"

Clara lost two relationships that week—Roger and Rita.

The best advice I can give you about giving advice is this: Don't give advice unless you are asked for it, and then really think about it and have the other person really think about it before you put your two cents in. Sometimes, as in the case of Rita and Clara, the other person asking for the advice won't like the advice you give them, and they may even turn on you. So you may want to preface your two cents with, "Are you sure you want to hear my honest opinion?" or "You may not like what you hear."

There will invariably be times when you feel compelled to give your advice even though the other person has not asked you for it. If you have to offer advice, couch it with, "It's only my opinion, but . . ." or "You can take this for whatever it's worth . . ." or "I don't want this to affect our relationship, but I want to give you my honest opinion . . ." or "I'm not an expert . . ." or "It's only one person's opinion . . ." This will give the other person room to reject your advice without rejecting you.

You *can* also offer advice, like criticism, even if you are not asked for it, but it is important that you offer the advice as a gesture of friendship and caring, with a sensitivity for the other person's feelings. In doing so, you must be willing to risk putting your friendship on the line.

The last thing you want to do is *force* advice on another person, though there are exceptions. For example, a hairdresser I know was telling me about how she took cocaine and got drunk the night before. As someone who has seen the devastating effects of drugs and alcohol I felt morally obligated to give the woman some advice, which was that she was flirting with death and with the possibility of having a stroke which could permanently affect her ability to speak. So I told her point blank—"Look, you are a beautiful woman with a lot going for you, but using drugs and alcohol is stupid and if you keep doing it, you have a good chance of either killing yourself or having a stroke. If that happens, you won't be able to walk or talk. So get some professional help and stop this stupidity." She was quiet and refused to speak to me. Finally three months later, she called to tell me that I was the catalyst that got her into a drug and alcohol rehabilitation program, which turned her life around. So there are times when you *must* give firm and honest advice, especially if it can save a person's life!

HONESTY IS YOUR BEST POLICY

People lie for different reasons—not to hurt the other person or to make someone feel good or to make themselves feel better and more important than they really are. Whatever the reason is that causes you to lie, it all boils down to a lack of self-esteem.

Your life can be so much easier when you confront what is true. Granted, for many, it's not always easy to tell the truth, but it's better to say nothing at all than to lie. Instead of lying, you don't have to answer a person's intrusive questions. You can say, "I can't answer that question," or "I'll be able to tell you about that later, when I have more to say," or "I'm not at liberty to discuss this with you."

As a communications specialist, I have on more than one occasion had to say to people, "I am sorry, but I am not at liberty to discuss that person with you." I set limits by not revealing *anything* about *anyone* because everything that goes on in my office is confidential. Throughout the years I've heard it all and have vicariously lived out thousands of fantasies through the lives of my clients; however, nobody will ever know the details but me.

One of my clients works in the lingerie department at a major department store and told me that one of her customers' husbands came into the store one day to buy lingerie—not for his wife or his mistress, but for himself (in an extra-large size). She was in a dilemma. Should she alert her steady customer as to what her husband was doing, or should she keep her mouth shut and say nothing? She decided to do the latter since her job was to sell lingerie and not make moral judgments or get involved in her customers' personal lives.

In close personal relationships, honesty is essential if you want to avoid being hurt. The most successful relationships I have seen are the ones where both parties "lay their cards out on the table" on a consistent basis and are completely honest with one another at all times.

Honesty really *is* also the best policy in the business world. Sure, almost everybody is out to make a deal. But most successful business people I have known, who have enjoyed forty or fifty or sixty years of prosperity, pride themselves on their "honesty." You have to be honest with your business associates to have the reputation to maintain your longevity in the business world. You have to maintain an integrity in order to maintain good business relations. When you have integrity you have self-respect and the respect of others. People enjoy doing business with people they *trust*.

Of course, there will always be people who find lying easier than telling the truth, and your best policy toward these people is to let them know that you're aware of their behavior or stop dealing with them. You don't have to attack them and call them a "dirty liar," but, instead, allow them to save face by saying something like, "I think there may be a discrepancy here."

How can you tell if someone is lying to you? There are signals. Dr. Paul Eckman of the University of California at San Francisco and author of a book on lying, informs us that only five percent of the people are skilled enough to lie and hide it, and for the rest there are give-away signals—telltale muscle movements and signs of emotions that people who are lying frequently try to conceal. So most of us usually know if someone is lying.

... 8 ...

Business Matters

Communicating in the business world is a lot different from communicating in your personal life because so much more is at stake. Unlike your personal life, where you can pick and choose whom you want to talk to, in the business world you have to be prepared to communicate with anyone. Your entire livelihood depends on your ability to communicate with your co-workers, your boss, your employees, your customers—anyone whom you come in contact with.

JOB INTERVIEWS

Allow the interviewer to take the lead. Take your cues from the interviewer in terms of where to go, when to shake hands, when to sit, and when to talk and when to listen. Always keep in mind that you are a guest in their office. Never go into any interview with a chip on your shoulder. Under no circumstances should you greet your prospective employer in a frenzy, even if you've had to rush.

On the other hand, don't let anyone abuse you. One of my clients, an actress, went to see a manager for possible representation, and he started yelling at her because she wore pants instead of a skirt to an interview with him. "Just a minute, sir," she said. "I'm here for you to judge my personality and my abilities as an actress, not to show you my legs. So we have nothing else to say to one another."

When someone puts you down or insults you, speak up and let them know that any derogatory comments about you are totally out of line and completely unacceptable.

A lot of books encourage you to ask as many questions as you like at a job interview and even try to make small talk with your interviewer, but what you *really* should do is sit and listen as much as possible. It is the interviewer's arena.

When you do talk, the best bit of advice on what to say is, as President John F. Kennedy once said, "Ask not what your country can do for you, but what you can do for your country." Instead of asking how much your job will pay, how many vacation days you will be getting, and what the benefits are, tell what you can do for the company. One of my clients was looking for a new account executive for her advertising company. What turned her off the most was that the applicant kept talking about how much the job paid and what the hours would be. Of course, these things are important, but they're certainly not the most important things to the interviewer. If someone came into my office and said, "Dr. Glass, I've worked with deaf children in a clinic for the past five years. I love children. I know your practice mostly concentrates on adults, but I'd love to help build up the children's part of your practice so your business can grow," I would hire that person in a heartbeat, rather than somebody who said, "Yes, I work with children, but I'd really rather work with your celebrity clientele." My practice works because of what I give to my clients, not what I take from them. And anyone who works with me has to share this same philosophy.

If you are going to ask questions of the interviewer, ask *intelligent* questions. One of my clients, Brian, has never been refused a job. Headhunters are constantly calling him and sending him out on interviews. What makes Brian so incredibly different is the way he prepares for an interview. Whenever he is sent out on an interview, Brian researches the company. He goes to the library, gets everything he can possibly get his hands on and reads about the company—its size, history, all of its services or product lines—and then he literally "knocks the socks off" the interviewer and impresses them with intelligent questions about the company.

Ask questions that are intelligent and meaningful to the company—questions that present you as someone who is interested in how *you* can help the company.

At the job interview you should say as little as possible, unless you are asked to say more. When an interviewer asks you a question like, "Tell me about your family," say, "I'm married, I have two children, and we have lived in the suburbs for five years." Don't go on and on and say, "I have two kids. One of them wants to apply to medical school." Don't talk about the personal aspects of your life. Keep it simple, and keep it to the point. Know your intention, like the actor who has to know his intention when he approaches a particular scene. Know why you are at this job interview. You're not there to impress, because you can't *impress*. All you can do is be *real* and be your best self.

Recently, I served as a judge at a Miss USA Pageant, where I had to interview fifty women for the *job* of being Miss USA. The one who won, Miss Texas, was far above the other contestants because she only spoke when she was spoken to, and she didn't go out of her way to be anything other than herself. She was one hundred percent real and situationally appropriate. She was a perfect example of *less is more*.

One final caution: Studies have shown that using profanity, or "four-letter words," during an interview can cost you a job. Dr. Larry Powell and his colleagues at Mississippi State University showed that using profanity in a job interview consistently made a negative impression on interviewers.

Your first reaction to this study might be, "Well, that's obvious. Of course, I'd never say a four-letter word during an interview."

On a conscious level you wouldn't, but if you are consistently using profanity as part of your daily speech pattern, it may become such an ingrained habit that you might slip, especially if you are with an interviewer whom you feel a special camaraderie with. However comfortable you feel with your interviewer, never forget that you are there for a job interview.

One of my clients, a personnel administrator for a Fortune 500 company, told me that she can't believe the profanity people use during job interviews. She fears their use of profanity in the workplace may cause potential embarrassment to the company. So even though my client is not a prude and has a high tolerance for people's lifestyles, she will never hire anyone who uses profanity during the interview.

To end an interview, again take your cue from the interviewer. If the interviewer stands up, obviously the interview has come to an end. Watch for body cues, such as fidgeting, loss of eye contact, extraneous body movement, re-shuffling of papers, including the closing of your file.

There are people who are very ignorant of these cues and lose a job in the very last moments of the interview because they have *overstayed* their *welcome*. You can literally talk you way into a job through the front door and out of a job through the back door. What you do and say at the end of the interview is just as important as what you say and do at the beginning of the interview.

So be aware of your actions. Be gracious and courteous when you leave and thank the person for the time they spent with you.

YOU AS THE INTERVIEWER

As the interviewer, you have to take all of your first impressions and prejudices and stick them in your back pocket. If somebody reminds you of your old boyfriend or has a shirt on that you don't like, or if they are wearing the same perfume as your ex-wife, get rid of your prejudices immediately.

Most of the time the person you are interviewing is going to be nervous. It's the nature of the situation. So it is up to you to try to make them feel comfortable and at home. Give them a little while to acclimate themselves. Try to include some benign chitchat about the weather, the traffic. Ask them if they want a cup of coffee or some water. Be a host and welcome them.

It's very important to be considerate, and even though you are busy and have a lot more people to interview, you owe it to the person to be respectful, kind, and not be abrupt with them. Don't use your position as a power trip. Also, don't talk about how busy you are—how many people you've seen or drop important names. The interviewee doesn't really care and, in fact, they may become depressed and feel more uncomfortable or feel their interview is a waste of time, that you are too busy for them. This may, in turn, be reflected in their attitude during the interview. They may not be their best self and may put out minimal energy and effort during the interview, thinking, "Well, they won't hire me anyway—the interview is obviously a waste of time so why bother."

If you are under pressure and need to end the interview more quickly than you would prefer, say, "I've really enjoyed this short time we've spent together. I feel I have a good sense of who you are and what your capabilities are. I don't mean to be rude, but I do have another commitment at this time. I truly have enjoyed our short time together and I will definitely get in touch with you."

And *definitely* get in touch with them. Never leave anyone hanging. If you don't want them for the job, let them know it soon. When you reject them, let them down gently. Tell the positive parts. For example: "You have many good qualifications and I am sure you are very capable. Unfortunately, we found someone else who is a little more suitable for our needs. We will keep your information in our files for the future in the event that further positions are available."

In Hollywood, oftentimes one hundred actors will apply for one acting position. Even though someone is rejected, if the casting agent or director says, "I loved how you did this scene," or "You are a terrific actor," this means a lot to the ego and to the self-esteem of a performer, and in some cases is almost as good as getting the job. So you may also want to say encouraging words to the people you have to let down.

TALKING TO YOUR BOSS

Many people have problems with authority figures. Some people are even belligerent toward people in positions of authority. One famous actor I know hates every director and producer he gets involved with. His fellow actors love him, because he doesn't have a problem with people who are not authority figures—he just has problems with people telling him what to do. As a result, he has developed a reputation for being a very difficult person to get along with and he has had difficulty getting work in Hollywood. If he wasn't such a gifted actor, many believe he wouldn't be getting any work at all.

If you aren't as lucky as this actor who gets hired despite his problem with authority figures, you may want to take care of it immediately by getting professional help. If you don't, it is a problem that can cost you a great deal.

It's very important to be able to get your point across when you talk to your boss, but you have to do it in a respectful manner. You have to understand that the *boss* is in charge. There is a reason for his authority, and he or she must be treated with respect. The Japanese have this down quite well—a person in a position of authority is bowed to a lot lower than a person who is not in a position of authority.

If you want to talk to your boss, make an appointment. Don't assume that you can just walk into your boss's office, because he or she may have other important things to deal with.

When you do talk to your boss, don't beat around the bush, don't chat, don't complain, just get to the point, without being emotional. Let's say one of your co-workers has a drinking problem, and because of this they have become an annoyance—they don't come to work on time, they're rude, they borrow materials and never return them, and they have been the cause of some severe technical errors that have cost the company money. You may want to preface your remarks by saying, "Ordinarily I would not bother you, but this particular situation has gotten so out of hand that I think it is affecting the company. I don't make it a habit of tattling on others, but it appears that one of our co-workers has a drinking problem. They have come late every day with alcohol on their breath, they have shown up drunk to sales meetings, and they have made some very severe technical errors that could be costing the company both money and customers. I am sorry to have to report this, but I felt it was necessary, for the good of the company."

You may also want to communicate to your boss through notes, because some bosses prefer communicating with you through memos so that all communication is documented. At

"Channel 7 Eyewitness News," where I served as health reporter, many talked to the bosses through memos. Find out what your boss prefers, and don't be afraid or embarrassed to approach them out of respect for both your cause and the company's. After you've gotten your point across, leave quickly. Many a good communication has been ruined by overstaying a welcome.

In bringing up concerns about your job, you don't want to come across like a whining baby. Instead, you want to come across with key "buzz" phrases like "What is going on is not in the company's best interest," or "I feel the job could be done better if . . ." If you want to make changes in how your job is structured, you may want to say, "I feel that I could be even more effective in helping if I worked this way . . ." In other words, when you bring up concerns, bring them up in a constructive, positive way that will help the company.

Even if you feel you are being taken advantage of, a positive approach can make the difference between a change for the better and no change at all. As an office assistant, Theresa was overworked. She was working the back office, the front office, doing the billing, the filing. Theresa was an assistant who needed an assistant, but her boss refused to give her one. Finally at the end of one long day, which ended for Theresa at midnight, she sat at her desk with tears running down her cheeks and realized that she had no life. The next morning, she went into her boss's office and said, "I realize we all have a lot of work to do, but I physically can't handle everything I am doing. I'm very efficient, but we really need to hire another person."

Of course, her boss balked. "I can't afford two secretaries," he said, but Theresa was ready for this. There were intern programs at the colleges, she told him, where students were sent out for on-the-job-training at no cost to the employer. She also suggested that instead of spending the "kitty" money every Friday for donuts, coffee, and refreshments for the weekly office party, it would be in the office's best interest if they used that money instead to pay a part-time college student to come in and help out with the work. The office parties could be reduced to once a month, and the several hours that had been wasted every Friday would be turned into productive work time.

Theresa's boss saw her point of view, and she wound up getting the help she needed. He saw her point because she had not become emotional, but was direct, positive, and to the point.

If you are overworked and underpaid, communicate loyalty to the company rather than complain. In most cases, when a boss sees loyalty, it's usually rewarded.

GETTING RECOGNITION

Many times you won't get recognition—and that's okay. After all, nobody asked you to work for recognition. As long as you recognize you've done a good job, that's what really matters.

On the other hand, when your recognition is being usurped by someone else, you have to stand up and claim the recognition you deserve. There are times when you must toot your own horn, when you can't be afraid to sing your own praises. If you are excited and proud of what you did, don't hesitate to share your excitement about how you were met with constant rejection but through perseverance and tenacity managed to get a particular account. Your success and excitement over your achievement will often motivate others around you as you become a catalyst to spark their excitement. So don't hesitate to let your boss know how you are supporting the company and are a team player, which can put you in an even better light in your company.

It takes a big person who has a healthy sense of self-esteem and security to openly recognize others at work who are doing well. It endears you to these people and shows a sense of camaraderie and openness. This recognition shouldn't be limited to your peers or co-workers, but should also be given to your boss as well. After all, your boss is human, too, and like the rest of us occasionally needs some recognition. If something your boss says or does moves or inspires you, don't hesitate to let your boss know in a sincere and honest manner.

ASKING FOR A RAISE

Before you ask your boss for a raise, you need to know the status of the company. If the company is going belly-up and there is a problem with finances, you need to know that. On the other hand, if you and John are doing the same job and you both have the same experience but you earn less, you have to ask for a raise.

You need to document why you merit receiving more money. Don't whine when you ask for a raise. Also, don't bring up your home expenses and your personal financial problems. It's such a turnoff for an employer to hear that you have to put your kid through school, or that you husband has been laid off. This has nothing to do with the work you are doing for the company. I can't stress enough that you need to leave your problems at home, whether you are talking about money or anything else.

If you really feel you are working hard and that you are not receiving the money you deserve, it may tell you something about your status at the company. For example, if you have been in a position for ten years and you are still making what you earned when you were first employed, that tells you a great deal. You may want to ask yourself: "Am I worth enough to this company?" You may even want to get another job in a similar position at another company where chance of advancement is better.

In order to approach your boss for a raise, there are several basic steps you need to follow. 1) Set up an appointment with your boss at their convenience. 2) Don't be outwardly nervous or shaking. Put your emotions in your pocket, and breathe out your tension. I keep stressing breathing exercises because they are the bible when it comes to eliminating stress. 3) Be specific and honest. Don't say, "I did *this*, so I deserve this amount of money." Instead say, "I've worked for this company for ten years. During this time I have brought in a lot of business, and I feel that I've been overlooked for a raise, so I would like to have a raise in my salary." 4) If you feel it is appropriate, offer to make the raise worth it for your boss by offering to take on extra responsibilities for the raise.

If you don't get the raise you are asking for, don't lose your temper. Don't curse or say, "How dare you! *So-and-so* got a raise!" When someone refuses to give you a raise, it most likely means one of two things: Either you are not worth that much to the company or they can't afford you. It's up to you to find another company where you will be worth more.

DEALING WITH A VERBALLY ABUSIVE BOSS

Throughout the years I have heard hundreds of stories about abusive bosses. The story is always the same: a mean, hypercritical, hostile boss who is taking his problems and hostilities out on the poor victims at work.

Bethany, who worked for a Fortune 500 company, was the scapegoat for everything that went wrong in her department because she was not willing to stand up to her boss. Instead of confronting him, she would tremble and cry whenever he became abusive. He knew he could get this reaction out of her, and that she would never quit. Bethany's problem was that her fuse was too long—she was willing to take too much.

In dealing with an abusive, critical boss, you have to make sure that your fuse is *short*. Make it known from day one—when the abusive-habit patterns are established—that you are not willing to take it. No job is worth disrespect, no matter how much money you get.

One of my clients, Richard, was constantly being singled out as a target for abuse by the president of his company. One day he was singled out and made a laughing stock on five separate occasions at one company meeting in front of all the other executives. Finally, he stood up in front of forty other executives and said, "I realize you are the president of this company, but under no circumstances will I be treated this way in front of my peers—or anybody for that matter. This is unacceptable behavior." He then sat down and not a word was uttered, and from that time on, his boss has a lot more respect for him.

If someone is verbally abusing you, it is up to you to tell them how to treat you. The minute you feel abuse coming, let them know "This is unacceptable." You have to set limits. You need to confront it in a concise and immediate manner. Get to the point, and then get back to work.

TALKING TO EMPLOYEES

When you talk to employees, you have to treat them with respect.

Dr. Robert J. Gorlin, one of my professors at the University of Minnesota, was and is one of the finest human beings I have ever met in my life, and a great mentor. He is also the best communicator I have ever known. Everybody loved being around Dr. Gorlin and working with him. He treated everybody with respect. His motto was: "A pat on the back is only a few vertebrae removed from a kick in the pants." Dr. Gorlin's lesson is a simple one: We should all treat one another with respect. We need to be kind and gentle to one another. Also, praise can motivate a person more than you can ever imagine.

There are many people who are gifted motivators as Dr. Gorlin is. They are so comfortable with themselves and have so much self-respect that they treat others—colleagues, superiors, or subordinates—with the respect and dignity that they deserve.

If you are talking to your secretary, don't be afraid to be enthusiastic, even when dictating a letter. Positive energy is both infectious and motivating. If somebody is having a problem in their personal life, don't just dismiss them by saying, "There is no room for personal problems here." What you want to say is, "If you are having a problem and you don't feel that you can continue working today, perhaps you would like to take the day off and make it up some other time." You can't be such a taskmaster that your employees are afraid of you. Although fear may be a way of keeping workers in line, many feel, and research shows, that people do not work well under negative pressure.

Once again, it is important to remember that if you want positive results you have to have a positive attitude toward people. When I worked at Channel 7 as a health reporter, there was a truly wonderful news producer named Charlie Darling. His name fit him. He was so positive and supportive to the reporters that everyone wanted to go out of their way for him. Whenever a job was well done, he took the time to let them know how well they had performed. The news business is most stressful and does not bring out the best personality traits in everyone. This unusual man made it a joy to work in television. He certainly is living proof of the "pat-on-the-back" philosophy.

There are, of course, times when people do not do the right thing, and when you have to give someone constructive criticism so they do the job right. Research has shown that there are key words and phrases when you are giving someone constructive criticism. They are: "Perhaps it would be a better idea . . ." or "You might try . . ." or "Why don't you consider . . ."

You need to be direct and set limits, but you need to do it in a positive way, allowing the other person to maintain their self-respect. The person needs to feel as though they are capable of improvement and that they are not a lost cause and in jeopardy of losing their job.

One of the things I have heard bosses say all too often is "That was horrible, disgusting, awful. You did a terrible job." This kind of behavior will neither win you respect nor will it influence people to do good work for you. People will not be motivated or influenced by this kind of criticism. If you do have to tell someone that they are not doing a good job, sit them down and give them alternatives, and let them know that you know they are capable of more.

HOW TO FIRE SOMEONE

On the other hand, there are times when as a boss you've tried different alternatives with your employee and nothing works. You just have to let them go.

Firing someone is probably the hardest thing you will ever have to do because being fired is the ultimate rejection. And yet, I know of incidents—particularly in the news and television business—where people have gone to work to find their names painted over on their parking spaces, or had their belongings removed by a security guard. This is inexcusable; it's unconscionable because it is so degrading.

When you fire someone, you don't want to generate hate and animosity because the person can retaliate—and often will! In fact, I know of one incident where a very deranged individual who was fired inappropriately and humiliated in front of everyone in the company (and was asked to leave the premises) saw to it that nobody else would leave that day. This man was obviously mentally disturbed, but he was sane enough to realize that murder was out of the question. Instead he said, "If they won't let me in, I won't let them out." Every morning there was a two-hour meeting in the conference room, after which everyone would go to lunch. During those two hours, he made sure no one would leave the office by cementing the doors to the conference room shut with a strong glue. Of course, we all remember the former disgruntled city councilman Dan White, who murdered fellow council member Harvey Milk and the mayor of San Francisco, George Moscone, out of anger over his dismissal.

If you have to fire someone, do it behind closed doors. In certain cases, it may be best to let people go immediately, as opposed to giving them notice. Whatever you do, you need to do it in a calm, civilized manner. It may even be best to do it in a letter or by a telephone call before the person comes to work. A client of mine was fired when he arrived at work after spending the morning doing his job. His boss just walked up to him with no explanation and flatly said, "You're fired." At first he thought his boss was kidding, until he realized that everyone else in the company knew that he was fired and treated him as though he had leprosy—they wouldn't even talk to him.

So if you must fire someone, you need to do it gently, carefully, and respectfully. You need to use one of the following alternatives: (1) Tell them their good points, that they are not a bad person but this job is not for them. Tell them you are sorry that their expertise doesn't seem to be working out *in this company.* (2) Tell them that your finances have made it necessary to cut back staff on the job. (3) Say, "We've had so many difficulties with one another that it appears that it would be better for both you and our company to go our separate ways."

Unless the person has cheated or stolen money from the company, or their lack of integrity has jeopardized the company, you may want to tell them that you would be more than happy to write them a letter of recommendation to assist them in getting another job.

COMMUNICATIONS PROBLEMS IN THE WORKPLACE

There are problems in any work environment. You can avoid many of these problems if you follow some simple rules of communicating.

MIXING BUSINESS WITH PLEASURE

Should you invite the boss home to dinner? Should you get an extra set of tickets and invite your co-workers to the Lakers game? My philosophy is that business and pleasure can be combined, but you have to set limits. Too often, when you are socializing, you let your hair down. Your language may be freer, your dress may be more casual, your likes and dislikes and opinions may reveal themselves, and you may even reveal your intimate secrets, especially after a few drinks.

There is no place for such freedom in the workplace because the old saying "Familiarity breeds contempt" often holds true and too much is at stake at work.

Doreen, an attorney, and Linda, her secretary, became very close friends. They were both single and boyfriendless. They would go out to the movies and out to drink in the evenings after work and even went shopping for clothes together. While spending so much time together, they also shared their most intimate secrets. Back at the job, Doreen, the attorney, was in a position to hire an executive secretary for one of the bosses of the company. Instead of filling the position with Linda, she hired an outsider. The reason she did not want to hire Linda was because they were such good friends and she didn't want to lose her companionship at work. On the other hand, this jeopardized Linda's opportunity for advancement and more pay, creating hard feelings. Unfortunately, Linda wasn't mature enough to tell her boss Doreen how devastated she was. Instead, she took it out on Doreen by spreading gossip about her love life and other secrets she had been told in confidence. So the expression "Never tell your best friend anything you wouldn't want your worst enemy to know" holds true in this case.

It's an insurance policy. You need to be on guard. Never share intimate feelings with co-workers that could potentially jeopardize your reputation at work. You can certainly share your viewpoints, but make sure you wouldn't mind anyone else knowing about them. Save special talk for your husband, your lover, your shrink, anybody out of your work environment, so that it won't ever be thrown in your face.

One of my clients who has a passion for Japanese women shared his fantasy with a colleague at work. Later, when a Japanese woman was hired as a secretary, his colleague made his life very uncomfortable. Whenever he would talk to the new secretary, the colleague would say—right in front of her—"Are you living out your fantasy? How are things in Fantasyland?" Besides embarrassing my client, this insensitive needling put a sour taste in everybody's mouth. When my client confronted his colleague, he was told, "Oh, I was just kidding."

Nobody can afford this kind of kidding in the workplace, because it diminishes your level of respect among your fellow employees. So never share your fantasies with anyone at work. Remember, you can mix business with pleasure, but make sure that you're in control. Be willing to accept the consequences if you share your intimacies at work.

There are, of course, some very close relationships between people that begin at work, but be aware that they can backfire, and there is more at stake than just a friendship.

GOOD OLD BOYS NETWORKS AND
POWDER ROOM CLIQUES

The "good old boys" network and the "powder room clique" are one and the same, only one is a man's club and the other is a woman's club. There are office cliques, and what you say to one person in one of these cliques will spread like wildfire and oftentimes will be distorted as it moves through the clique.

One of my clients, Shiela, experienced this. She had a date with her boss. Everybody liked both of them individually, but when she confided to one of her fellow workers that they were an item, she was suddenly branded an "opportunist," a "slut," as gossip spread through the office. Earlier that morning, everyone was smiling and friendly to her, but in a matter of an hour she noticed people not giving her eye contact and avoiding her.

We've all heard the expression "Misery loves company." If you are stuck in a poor job situation or can't find the right love of your life, it may feel better sharing your blues with your comrades at work who are in the same boat. But when your life finally does take a big turn for the better, it may be in your best interest not to share all of your good fortune with your co-workers, lest they feel a tinge of jealousy. This happened to Steve, a client of mine.

Steve had not been in a relationship with a woman for ten years. He was extremely overweight and had been in a bad marriage. He had just given up on women and dedicated himself to his work. One day, at an office party he met Karen and they literally fell in love. At first, all of his drinking buddies at work were happy for Steve, but then they noticed a change in him—he was too happy for their liking. Suddenly, he was always smiling, he stopped complaining about how miserable life was, he took off thirty pounds, stopped smoking and stopped drinking. In essence, he was no more fun to his work buddies. Even though the relationship between Steve and Karen became stronger, he stopped sharing his joy with people at work. When his buddies asked him how his relationship was working out, he told them the truth, but didn't overdo it—that they were getting along okay and were really good friends. Suddenly he noticed all the guys smiling, patting him on the back and saying, "So, another one didn't work out. That's the breaks."

Steve learned a lot from this experience. He learned to keep his mouth shut about his personal life at work. Although he no longer drinks with the good old boys and has become more distant in his relationship with them, they still feel better about him because they don't know how really happy he is.

Not only do people at work not want to hear about your happiness, they also don't want to hear about your misery. What you say to your fellow employees can impair your credibility and create a lack of trust.

This happened to a stockbroker client of mine who was married to a beautiful model with a drug problem. He would come into my office and share with me the details of their horrible fights—how he found her with another man, how she jumped out of his moving car one night, how she caused a scene in the street when she hit him over the head with a bottle of water. It was okay that he shared this information with me because it would definitely not go beyond my lips. However, he was telling everyone else, even everyone at work, this same story. This came back to haunt him. His business went downhill because his customers no longer trusted him. When he came in bedraggled one morning after an all-night fight, his boss threw his family problems back at him, saying, "That druggie wife of yours may wind up costing you your job."

Suddenly, my client's eyes opened up. He realized that he had put himself in a position where his life had literally become a Peyton Place. He was eventually forced to change companies, but he learned from his mistakes. Now he keeps his mouth shut at work about his personal life.

Leave your personal problems outside the office door. Just do your job and treat yourself with the respect you deserve from others.

The best policy is never to be a part of office gossip. Even if you don't become an active participant, and you just listen, you may be blamed for spreading the gossip.

One of my famous-actor clients was called on the carpet by a studio executive one day for spreading gossip about a studio actress. All he had done in reality was just laugh at the gossip when he heard it. Somehow the gossip had been attributed to him when in reality he had only been a listener. He tried to defend himself, but the studio executive wouldn't believe him. From that time on, whenever he heard gossip or someone being trashed, he fled the scene.

So don't participate in office gossip under any circumstances, because one way or another it will usually come back to haunt you.

ARGUMENTS IN THE WORKPLACE

Obviously, if creative people get together in the workplace there are bound to be creative differences. Arguments will arise. But you don't have to fly off the handle. You have to express yourself appropriately and intelligently. In chapter 14, you will learn more about arguing in greater detail. However, in the work force, one of the most important things is not to let animosity build up. You need to deal with any problem as soon as it arises. If you don't like the way someone is talking to you, stop them immediately and say, "I don't like the way you are talking to me." Nip it in the bud as soon as possible so that they will know their limits.

SEXUAL HARASSMENT

There is no room in the workplace for sexual harassment—of either sex. There are both men and women who sexually harass workers and this needs to be stopped immediately.

Flirting oftentimes can make life more exciting in the workplace. Sometimes, if you have a crush or a fantasy about someone, it may even make you work harder. There is nothing wrong with fantasizing or flirting, as long as it doesn't get out of hand. But if it does, you need to protect yourself by speaking up immediately. You don't want to let this go on and on and then six months later complain about the fact that you are being sexually harassed, and maybe even find yourself embroiled in a sexual-harassment suit.

Men can also be victims of sexual harassment. A client of mine worked in a company where his boss, fifteen years his senior, took a liking to him and began flirting with him. He didn't realize he was being sexually harassed—he even encouraged the flirting at times—until things got out of hand and she began making sexual overtures toward him. When he rejected her advances, she was embarrassed and fired him. She told him she was quite surprised—after all, she felt, he had been encouraging her flirtations. Had this gentleman spoken up immediately and not encouraged her, no misunderstanding would have occurred and he would still have his job.

Unfortunately, there may be another side to sexual harassment, and that may be to ask yourself if you, indeed, have done anything to instigate this type of behavior. In one case a woman was very attracted to an executive in her company and she would constantly flirt with him. He ignored her advances, until one day he decided to take her up on her non-verbal overtures. As soon as he approached her directly, she started telling everybody at work that he was sexually harassing her. He was shocked. All he had done was follow her lead, and now he had to contend with a company investigation for sexual harassment.

Even though it may seem to be a rare incident, it is not. You have to be extremely careful—and direct—when you feel you are being sexually led on. He could have avoided the entire mess by directly confronting her and saying "Look, I've noticed you flirting with me, and although I find you attractive, I never get involved with anyone I work with."

It's very important not to send out the wrong signals. Watch how you dress and your movement when you are relating to others at work. There are those who will say, "This is a free country. Why can't I dress or move the way I want?" You certainly can in your private life. But in the work place, there are certain mores that you have to follow if you want to be successful.

Remember, just be direct when you deal with others, and don't start anything you can't finish.

OFFICE JEALOUSY

Oftentimes companies will create competition between co-workers. In essence, they will breed jealousy in order to make their employees work harder. I think this is an awful way to motivate people. It creates paranoia and fear in the work environment.

I took a survey and asked people if they would consider themselves to be jealous people. Close to eighty-five percent of the people I surveyed said that they definitely were not jealous. However, if you put any of these people in an unfair work situation where someone is getting more specialized treatment for whatever reason, the green-eyed monster will suddenly appear. When this happens it breeds contempt for the person who is unfairly winning and for the company.

There are people who get off easy. One of my clients was working on her doctoral degree in psychology. She was one of two female doctoral candidates in the department, and was having a terrible time with her committee members due to the politics involved. The other woman in her department had no difficulty at all, mainly because she was sleeping with an advisor. This bred a lot of ill will and jealousy on the part of my client. She felt that the whole situation was extremely unfair and became so depressed that she ended up hating everybody—

the other female doctoral candidate, her own advisor, and even the university—and her performance suffered. Through realizing that her jealousy was self-destructive and non-productive, she was eventually able to confront the powers that be and get her degree.

Jealousy can impede your performance if you are in an unfair environment. You need to confront the powers that be in the unfair situation. If you are in a work situation where you are being clearly overlooked and someone else is being treated with unfair favoritism, don't let your jealousy get the best of you. Either confront the situation or leave for the sake of your own mental health.

What if somebody is jealous of you? There are those who will ignore it and say, "Oh, that's their problem." But unfortunately you can't always ignore someone's hostile actions due to their feeling threatened by or jealous of you. It's difficult to be around a person who is not truly happy for your success. People who are jealous of you will often sabotage your efforts and try to make you look bad. When this happens, the only thing you can do is to directly question their motives in order to let them know that you are aware of what they are doing and that their behavior is unacceptable to you.

SECRETS OF GREAT BUSINESS COMMUNICATORS

Throughout my years of experience in my private practice, I've been fortunate enough to meet some of the most prominent and successful leaders in the business world. From my many hours of talking to them I've learned a great deal about why these people are so successful. I've discovered that they all possess a common trait that enabled them to be as successful as they are. This common denominator is that they are *excellent communicators*. They know how to talk to people and how to get what they want.

I have learned that great leaders shared seven traits that contributed to their success.

1. They were confident and never afraid to ask for what they wanted.

2. They appreciated people when they did get them what they wanted.

3. They consistently nurtured relationships and maintained open lines of communication—not only when they wanted something from that person.

4. They were tenacious. They never gave up. They just tried another route or strategy to achieve their goals.

5. They were excellent listeners. They didn't shut people out, kept an open objective mind, and listened to the negative as well as the positive.

6. They bounced back quickly from rejection or depression. This was reflected in the tone of their voice and their attitude. If they were upset about something someone had said to them earlier that day, they didn't carry it with them their entire day.

7. Finally, they were friendly and approachable. They said hello to employees they came into contact with. They weren't stingy with their praise and gave well-deserved pats on the back.

If you do these seven things, you too have the chance to become one of the best communicators in your business. You'll not only find that your relationships with co-workers and clients will improve, but that you feel happier and have an increased sense of confidence and self-esteem.

... 9 ...

Social Savvy

There is a joy in going to parties and giving parties. Parties are by far the best way to meet people, to get to know people better, and to cement existing relationships. This chapter will focus on how to talk to people at parties, how to act at parties, and how you can use a party to your best advantage and feel more comfortable at parties.

HOSTING A PARTY

There are many people who hate to give parties because to them it is stressful. My feeling is that there are *no* hard, fast rules for party-giving. However, there are rules for being a good host or hostess. If people had a good time at a party, they're not going to remember if the silverware was lined up properly or what you wore. What they *are* going to remember is if you—the host or hostess—made them feel comfortable, and if they met some people they liked and "connected" with at the party.

There can be a lot of personal fulfillment in being a good party host because it gives you the opportunity to network—to get people together who can help each other socially, personally, and professionally.

Oftentimes, the associative property that we learned in high school algebra applies: if A = B and if B = C, then A = C. What we mean by this is, if you like the people you are inviting to your party, chances are they are going to like each other as well, because they like *you*, and *you* are the common likeable link.

At the most memorable parties I have been to the host or hostess has been warm and gracious and has had things under control.

Ten years ago, when I first came to Los Angeles, I attended a party at a man's home who made me and the other guests feel that we were the most important people in the world. He not only cooked dinner, but was a great conversationalist. He got everyone involved in the conversation, and he made sure that everybody's needs were met—that we were comfortable and that we all had enough to eat and drink. He even played the piano to entertain us. I have never forgotten this party or the warmth of this wonderful man who welcomed me into his home. His hosting ability was just a glimpse of who he was as a person. It was a microcosm of his warmth and generosity. When I watched the Academy Awards in 1988 and watched Arnold Kopelson receive the Academy Award for producing the film *Platoon*, I wasn't surprised. I realized that only a person with enormous personal power could bring the right people together to accomplish such a task. He'd made wonderful things happen like he did ten years earlier when he "produced" a memorable dinner party.

Georgia Frontieri is not only known for ownership of the Los Angeles Rams and her opera singing, she is also known for being a lovely, gracious hostess. She introduces top people from the fields of business, sports, politics, and entertainment to one another—people who would not ordinarily meet one another. The conversation is always fascinating and stimulating, because as a wonderful hostess, Georgia knows how to bring out people's strengths and interests.

INTRODUCING YOUR GUESTS TO ONE ANOTHER

One of the most crucial elements of a successful party is introducing your guests to one another. As I discussed in chapter 1, when you introduce two people, don't just say, "Rebecca, this is Mary Thompson." Go into detail. Say, "Rebecca, I would like you to meet Mary Thompson. Mary has been in advertising for years and lives in the same part of town that you do." Try to find a common ground on which to connect your guests.

Don't be afraid to *talk up* your guests when you introduce them. Instead of saying, "This is John. He is a tax attorney," give him a little PR: "This is John. He is one of the most prominent tax attorneys in the city." If you notice that a person is getting embarrassed, say, "I don't want to embarrass John, but he is great. He was educated at Yale and supports a lot of the causes you are interested in."

By saying "Mary is an actress. She was in the movie . . ." you save people the embarrassment of having to ask, "What movie were you in? Where did I see you?" Tell them what movie she was in and let them know how much you enjoyed her performance. It's very important to talk up your guests. So don't be afraid to build them up along with their achievements.

The most important thing you can do is to make yourself available for your guests. If you notice that Don is not getting along with Julie or he is all alone, make sure that he is taken care of by introducing him to someone else.

It is your obligation to make people feel at home, to control the environment as best you can so that your guests will feel as comfortable as possible. You need to make sure that people are constantly meeting other people, that their needs are met, and that they are having a good time. You also need to ask people from time to time if they are having a good time or if there is somebody else they would like to meet.

Ideally, the host needs to introduce all guests to one another. If this isn't possible due to logistics, the host needs to assign a co-host to help with this task. In essence, everyone has to meet everyone else. It is best to introduce a person as soon as they walk into the room. We've all seen movies of very formal black-tie events where royalty was introduced with trumpets and fanfare as they walked down a long red carpet as their name was announced. This may be a bit extravagant for parties. However, the concept of introducing each person individually as they enter the room is a wonderful one. Instead of trumpets, you may want to stand at the door and announce your guests as they arrive or have your co-host do this task if there are too many guests for you to handle. You need to welcome your guests and then turn to your other guests and say, "Everyone, I'd like you to meet my friend Mindy who flew in from Minneapolis."

By doing this, you have let everyone know who you guests are and a little something about them, so other guests can find common ground to talk about to that person during the party.

GAMES AND ATTRACTIONS

Party games may be a good way of opening communication channels between guests. However, one's guests might feel self-conscious participating, so don't make them. Though you've arranged for games to be played, don't be insistent on having guests participate. This creates resentment. It depends on the mood of the party and how the guests are feeling at the time. Before announcing a party game will begin, take an informal survey among the guests and ask if they would like to participate. If not enough wish to play, don't force anyone—forget it.

If you are hosting a party, you may instead want to have some sort of creative activity your guests can share in, like an artist drawing caricatures of your guests or a magician-comedian-astrologer or psychic. A karioke party where everyone gets up and sings can also be fun. These unique activities can lead to further conversation, and can be entertainment that can be the catalyst for stimulating further conversation among your guests.

SEATING ARRANGEMENTS

The biggest insult you can inflict on a person, especially at a sit-down dinner party, is seating them next to someone who is totally inappropriate for them to meet. This happened to a friend of mine. Claire is a single, attractive woman, and the hostess knew that. Even though there were several single, attractive men at the table, she put her right between two unavailable men—a gay lawyer and a gay architect. Claire was disappointed, because she wanted to meet some attractive, single, *available* men. She didn't have anything in common with either of these men, who ended up ignoring her and talking to one another over her. Finally, she said, "Would you two prefer sitting next to each other?" to which they answered yes. After they changed seats and treated her as though she wasn't there, she was seated next to a lecherous married man who kept trying to seduce her, even though his wife was sitting right next to him! It is obvious that the hostess didn't put much thought into the seating arrangements. Claire got the message that she wasn't that important to her hostess, even though she enticed her to come to the party by telling her she was going to introduce her to some great guys. In seating your guests, pay close attention to what your guests' needs are and who has something in common with whom. You may even want to let them know ahead of time you may be putting them next to someone they may get along with or may want to meet. You can even ask your guests whom they would like to sit next to.

DEALING WITH RUDE, OUT-OF-CONTROL GUESTS

Whenever you are faced with a rude guest, or one that is out of control, you need to let them know immediately that their behavior is not acceptable. Carol was having a good time at her own party until her friend Debby started cutting her down for no reason with sarcastic remarks like "Oh, I didn't know you cooked." Pretty soon the sarcasm became contagious. Carol's other friends, who had previously never said anything sarcastic to her, starting picking on Carol and teasing her. It was obvious that she was becoming more and more uncomfortable at her own party. Finally, she said, "Debby, why don't you just stop it. I'm trying to have a nice dinner party and there is no room for sarcasm here." At first there was a nervous silence in the room but after a few moments, everyone relaxed and the conversation returned to normal—without the sarcasm.

Even though the joking had been in fun, Carol's guest were able to see from her remark that it had been hurting her. She had let them know that it had got out of hand and that this was not how she wanted people to act in her home.

If someone is ruining your party by being sarcastic or obnoxious, you need to let them know immediately that their behavior is not acceptable. You can take them aside and tell them privately, or you may want to do it right in front of everyone, because perhaps that is the only way they will get the message.

If someone is out of control, you need to ask them to leave, but do it firmly and gently. They may have had too much to drink and they may not be aware of how obnoxious they are acting.

Just say, "You appear to have had a little too much to drink. It's probably a good idea for you to go home now." If they are drunk, be sure to call them a cab to get them home safely. Although it may be a very sticky situation, you have to confront these people immediately. Otherwise, the situation can get out of hand. You need to get rid of any toxic element that can affect the mood of your party. An unhappy situation, like having an obnoxious guest present, can be infectious and put the other guests off and, in essence, ruin your party.

GIFTS

Whenever people attend a party, they should bring a gift. It doesn't have to be an expensive gift, but a meaningful gift—a bottle of wine, a box of chocolates, or a dessert is a good way for a guest to let their host know that they appreciate being invited to their party.

When a guest is appreciative enough to make such a gesture, don't say, "Oh, you shouldn't have." Just let them know that their gift is appreciated and thank them graciously.

If it's a birthday party and they bring you a birthday gift, let them know how much you appreciate their gift, and open the gift at the party, unless they ask you not to. (Always be sure to write a thank-you note to the person and send it to them as soon as possible.)

It may also be a nice gesture on the part of the host to give the guests little gifts as well. It shows a lot of class and thoughtfulness. This is especially true at a sit-down dinner, when a gift should be given to each of the guests. It could be a simple flower at each table, or a special object. The guests should be appreciative when they take their party favors home and not forget to thank the host for the gift and express how much they like it—if in fact they do.

In some social circles, not showing up at a party can be the end of a relationship. People take your lack of attendance as a personal affront—especially if you've said you would attend and then don't. If you do accept the invitation, make sure you are there. If, at the last minute, something has come up, call the host immediately and express your disappointment. The next day, follow up your call with another call as well as with a gift, and be honest. Reiterate your disappointment at not being able to attend. If you know a day in advance that you won't be able to attend a party, you need to tell your host or hostess why you can't attend—especially if the person is a friend. Don't lie. Don't say you've got to go out of town when you really do not have to. If your host eventually finds out you weren't out of town and you told a "white lie," that may cost you a friendship because you have broken the trust between you.

WHEN YOU CAN'T ATTEND

There are many reasons why you might not be able to attend a party:

1. Perhaps you have another obligation.
2. You've had enough of your host's parties and you're not eager to see the same boring people or eat the same boring food.
3. You are feeling bad about yourself because you've gained weight and don't want to hear everyone's comments about how you've "put on a little weight," or worse, not hear the comments of how great you look.
4. You're extremely tired and don't feel like going out.
5. You're uncomfortable about meeting any new people.
6. You're on a strict diet and know that if there is food around, "you'll just have to eat it."
7. You have no way of getting there.
8. You're unable to find a friend or an escort to go with you, and you're self-conscious about coming alone.
9. You don't feel well: You may have an upset stomach and feel lethargic and just don't feel like being around other people.

10. You may not like the other guests, the host, their spouse, or anyone else attending the party.

11. You don't like mixing business with pleasure and feel uncomfortable attending the party.

12. You completely forgot about it.

Although it's in your best interest to always be honest about why you can't attend a party, some of these reasons listed above may offend the host. Your best excuse is that you have other plans or that you're just not feeling up to the occasion.

Sometimes, if you are completely honest and say that the reason you don't want to attend is that you are on a strict diet, or that you can't find transportation or feel uncomfortable coming alone, you may find that the host or hostess can accommodate you by helping you to monitor your food intake, getting you transportation, or arranging for somebody to come to the party with you.

Many hosts and hostesses are very understanding if you are completely honest with them and tell them that you don't feel very good about yourself and don't feel in the mood to go out, or that you are a homebody lately, or that there will be people at the party that you will feel uncomfortable around, or finally, that you feel uncomfortable mixing business with pleasure. On the other hand, you don't want to hurt your host's or hostess's feelings by telling them that their parties are always boring and that you really don't feel like being in their company, when you decline their invitation.

Usually, when someone has asked you to a party a number of times and you constantly say no, they will often get the message. If they don't, just keep refusing. If they're bold enough to keep asking, continue to be bold enough to refuse.

What do you do if you actually forget to attend a party or show up on the wrong day? I was recently invited to a surprise birthday party for a deaf girlfriend of mine, which I was sure was on Saturday at 10:00 P.M. I invited a handsome young man to go with me as I was fixing my friend up with him as a surprise birthday "gift" to her. When we approached the house, it was very quiet. This didn't bother me because I figured that there were a lot of deaf people there and it would be a quiet party. As I approached the house, everything was dark as well as quiet. After banging on doors and creating a ruckus, the owner of the house, who was the supposed host, clad in his pajamas, proceeded to tell me that I came on the wrong day.

I wasn't able to attend the party on Sunday but left a note with my story about coming on the wrong day. This endeared me not only to the host but to my friend whose birthday it was.

If you absolutely forget a party, let the person know you forgot as soon as you remember. Send a gift along with sincere apologies and be completely honest so they won't take offense.

Helen, one of my clients, planned a birthday party on a day that her friend Tanya would have the time to attend. Tanya didn't show up at the party because she completely forgot. When Tanya did remember, she called—four days later—and casually mentioned to Helen that she forgot the party. She didn't show any remorse or emotion and didn't even send a gift to express her embarrassment or friendship, for that matter. Her lack of party etiquette ended their ten-year friendship.

People do take their parties seriously, especially if they are putting out money for food and entertainment, in addition to the time they spend planning the party. If you say you will come to their party—go. If you can't show up or you genuinely do forget, make it up to them by sending a gift immediately with a note expressing your regrets. This shows a lot of class and respect for the other person.

PARTY TALK

A lot of times people will tell me that they are going to an important party and they are nervous about what they are going to talk about. They are worried about who will talk to them, about how much time they should spend talking to a person, and what to do if nobody talks to them. This is one of the biggest fears people have. You're not alone if you have any of these fears, because at one time or another everyone feels insecure when they are going to a party, especially if they don't know many of the people who are going to be there.

The first person you are going to be talking to is obviously the host or hostess. It's very important to realize that the host or hostess is busy, so don't hog their time. Be very aware of the time that you do spend with them, and don't be offended if they don't spend a lot of time with you. If you really want to have a conversation with them, you may want to say, "I really want to spend some time talking with you, but I realize that you are very busy right now and it's not the time, so let's meet for lunch next week."

In general, this is a good thing to say to anyone you meet at a party whom you hit it off with. A party is a place to touch base with people, not to carry on deep, intense discussions. On the other hand, there may be some people whom you do connect with, but if you spend all your time with them, you will miss out on being a "part" of the party. There is nothing more disconcerting than to see two people at a party huddled in a corner ignoring everyone else in the room. Remember you are invited to a party, so partake and be a part of the party.

Body language is one of the most all-telling signals in terms of whether or not a person wants to talk to you, or whether or not you want to talk to them. On the other hand, if a person looks closed off, in terms of their body language, they may be giving off a wrong signal. They may just be shy or intimidated, so you may want to go over and start talking to them. If your comment or your reception is met with coldness, then your initial perception of the person is correct—but at least you tried.

What do you say to strangers you meet at a party? There are a lot of icebreakers. You can talk about the host, where the party is, when you got there, where you met the host, and why you showed up at the party. When you are in doubt about what to say or ask, remember what you learned in your high-school English class or in your journalism class—who, what, when, where, and why. Here are some good party ice-breaker questions:

- "How do you know the host?"
- "How long have you known the host?"
- "How did you meet?"
- "When did you get here?"

If you are eating food and drinking, you may want to engage the other person with, "Have you tried the quiche?" or "Would you like me to get you a drink?" This is a very endearing and kind gesture and shows that you are a giving person—someone who is not selfish and who is concerned about other people.

In order to engage in party conversation, you may want to talk about the events of the day. That's why I strongly encourage people to read the newspaper and even watch the news broadcasts just before going to the party so it will be fresh in your memory.

Under no circumstances are you to use "lines" in approaching someone at a party. We've all heard them, and most people are totally turned off by them. Saying, "You're the only ten in this room," or "You're so beautiful, are you an actress?" or "What's your sign?" are total turnoffs.

Other turnoffs are being too "nosy" or too invasive. For example, if somebody has just lost their job, don't pry by asking them what their boss said when he called them in and what their family is going to do now that they don't have a job. Nobody wants to be pressed for the gory details, no matter how interesting it may seem to the other person.

There are so many other things to say to a person that are real, honest, and endearing. There are people whom you may hit it off with immediately, at first glance. There are others who may want nothing to do with you, which may not be your fault at all. Look for conversational openers that are honest. You can talk about the weather, something you've just read in a magazine, what type of day it is, an interesting fact you've heard, something about your pet, or even a joke you've heard. Make sure, of course, it's a clean joke and not something that would embarrass you or the other person.

BEING SHY AT A PARTY

What you say in the first few minutes of meeting somebody reveals a lot about you. If you feel that you are shy, you need to get some help from either a psychologist or a communications specialist. You need to learn to get out of your own way and stop playing the *I think that you think that I think* game that we've talked about in earlier chapters. It can be the biggest handicap ever.

In my experience, I have found that most people who are shy have a tendency to be rather selfish: They are so consumed with how they are coming across that they lose sight of the purpose of the party, which is to meet people and have a good time. If you are shy, you need to take a breath in, hold it, let it out, and go up to a person and try to talk to them. The more you do it, the better off you'll be. Your first worry might be that you don't know what to ask the person. As long as you're not intrusive and ask them intimate questions initially, you have nothing to worry about. Ask their opinions about things. Just remember to get out of your own way and remind yourself that you are there to have a good time. It's not brain surgery you're going to. It's a party, so lighten up, and party!

TALKING TO PEOPLE WITH WHOM
YOU HAVE NOTHING IN COMMON

As long as you are a breathing human being and living on the planet Earth, you will always have at least one thing in common with another person.

The key is to find as much common ground as possible. The only way that you can do this is by asking questions and trying to be more *interested* than *interesting*.

Even if you find that you don't have a lot in common with someone, keep talking to them. Ask questions. You might learn something. Phrases such as "I'd like to learn more about it," or "Tell me more," or "That's interesting: I'm not familiar with it," or "Explain that to me," help you elicit more information from a person.

Let's say you meet a dentist and you feel that you have nothing to talk about. Well, if you have your teeth in your mouth, you have something to say. You may want to ask them if they know your dentist, where they got their training, how they got interested in dentistry, how they feel their profession has changed in the past few years. You can really relate to any-body—even someone who has been in prison. Even though you may feel like the two of you are worlds apart, which you probably are, it may be interesting to find out what their life was like in jail, providing they want to talk about it.

Most of the time, we feel we have little or nothing in common with somebody because we really don't know that much about the person. We haven't taken the time to find out enough about them to find a common thread. No matter what culture you are from, there are always things that can bond you to another person—family, friends, food, etc. Oftentimes, if a person is very different from you, they are even more fascinating to talk to.

NEGATIVE PARTY TALK

Have you ever been to a party and heard another person say, "Can you believe the dress that lady has on?" or "Doesn't that man look strange?" Danielle, an attractive businesswoman client of mine, was at a party and was standing next to the food table munching away when a man came up to her and said, "This food is so awful. This looks so bad. I can't believe the people at this party. They're so weird. Look at that man over there. He looks like a moose. He must be over three hundred pounds." Finally, my client turned to him and said, "You must be a very unhappy person, because all you seem to see is what is awful around here." Even though this man may have felt insecure at this party, negative small talk was not a way to attract people and encourage further communication. My client did the right thing. In cutting this man off, she was cutting the negative energy that was coming her way, because she was actually having a good time at this party.

WHAT TO SAY IN UNCOMFORTABLE SITUATIONS

While opening presents at her birthday party, a friend of mine was perspiring, so she took the wrapping paper and wiped her face and chest with it. One of her other guests yelled out, "Susan!" and gave her a look of disdain for not being ladylike. Susan stopped what she was doing, looked right at the woman, and said, "What do you want me to do—sweat all over my presents?" Perhaps it wasn't ladylike, but it was not this woman's place to reprimand the excited party girl, especially in front of other guests. So you need to put a lid on anyone who makes you uncomfortable or invades your space.

What if your ex-boyfriend or girlfriend or ex-mate shows up at a party? How do you handle that situation? There are three options. You can either leave the room, leave the party, or take a breath in, hold it, and confront the situation. Whatever you do, though, don't cause a scene. You may *want* to cause a scene if you see your boyfriend there with another woman, but *don't do it*. It's always best to be the classy lady or the gentleman you are and maintain your dignity at all times.

We've all witnessed scenes that are quite embarrassing. In fact, most of us live through these scenes vicariously. We can all relate to that person who did us wrong, who two-timed us, who cheated on us, and we all want our vicarious revenge.

I once attended a gallery opening where a woman unexpectedly saw the man she was supposedly exclusively dating with another woman. At first she was in complete shock, as she had spoken to him earlier that day and he told her he had a business meeting that evening. She was planning to stay home and relax when her best friend called to invite her. After her initial shock, she went into denial—that this beautiful woman he was with may very well have been a business associate—until she noticed how chummy they were with one another. The two-timed woman threw a drink at him, spat in his face, and started screaming, calling him various obscene names. She ran out of the party crying with her boyfriend running after her as the guests started to applaud. Then they all turned to stare at the other woman who by that point was looking rather sheepish. As the crowd broke up, many guests scurried outside to see what else would happen with the couple. Others began to laugh and discuss what they would have done if it had happened to them.

Even though you might feel like creating a scene, in the long run it's not in your best interest to create such a scene. You want to be a lady or a gentleman, as difficult as it may seem at the time. If you are unable to control yourself, leave the party. Wait until later, when you are more under control and in appropriate surroundings to confront your mate. Otherwise, it may even come back to haunt you.

UNCOMFORTABLE PARTY TALK

Let's say someone accidentally spills a drink on you or steps on your toe to the extent you think it is broken. What do you do when you feel violated? You need to be honest with your reactions and let the person know you are genuinely upset. Sometimes people are unaware that they've even injured you or spilled something on you. You don't have to be abusive or start pushing them or cursing at them. When they become aware of what has happened to you, most people will feel terrible about it. They will usually offer to pay for the dry cleaning or ask if you need medical attention. If they don't do this and you feel it's appropriate for them to make restitution, ask them where you can send the dry cleaning or medical bill.

If someone is rude—interrupts you, leaves you out of a conversation, is patronizing, or tells an offensive joke—you need to let them know immediately that their communication is unacceptable to you.

For example, let's say you're in the middle of telling a story and someone ignores you and interrupts you. You need to take a breath in, hold it for a few seconds, and look in their direction. In a bold, resonant tone, say, "Let me finish what I have to say before you go on." In essence, you're getting the "floor" as well as your "power" self-esteem back as you take control of the situation and not let the person walk all over you. The same holds true if someone is being rude, condescending, or putting you down. You need to look them in the eye and in your bold, resonant tone tell them that you don't appreciate the manner in which they are speaking to you. All too often, people tolerate others' insensitivities. They keep it in and harbor ill feelings as they walk away, taking the abuse without speaking up. Each time they do this it chips away at their self-esteem. By letting others know how you wish to be spoken to, you set the stage for a higher standard of communication.

This holds true for people who insist on telling jokes in poor taste that are offensive. If you are offended and sense an off-color or ethnic joke coming on, don't hesitate to interrupt that person in the middle of the joke by saying, "Oh, come on, we've heard enough of those type of jokes." Even though it may seem rude to cut them off, you may be doing them as well as yourself a favor by saving them possible embarrassment.

What do you do if someone is *too* friendly—a chatterbox who tries to "hang" onto you throughout the entire party? Most people don't want to be rude so they tolerate this person who has literally become a "pest" to them. In essence, the "pest" is usually unaware of how rude and inconsiderate they are being in taking up your time. Because you have allowed yourself to be victimized by this person, you often go away from the party feeling as though you've had a bad time. It's up to you to put a stop to a "hanger-on" or a "pest." Just look at them, smile, and say, "It's been nice talking to you," or "I've enjoyed meeting you but I'd like to circulate and meet some other people now." It's not necessary to ask them for their card or phone number just to be polite. Just smile and leave.

Sometimes the mood at a party is rather cold or unfriendly. You may find that everyone seems to know everyone else except you, and that people aren't warm. You may have even experienced situations where the guests seem somewhat "snobby," "cliquish," look down on you, or won't respond to any of your opening lines or friendly gestures. My advice is to keep trying to be friendly and try to connect with at least one person by smiling or making eye contact. If you've been milling around for over an hour and you've still gotten nowhere, then leave. You're probably at the wrong party.

There are a lot of people who are virtual magnets when it comes to attracting people and drawing them out. You, too, can be a magnet. This is not a difficult thing to learn. All you need to do is get out of your own way, look for the good in the other person, and tell them how you feel about them. Tell them how their work has affected you, tell them how they have inspired you. In essence, let them know that you appreciate them and that you are *interested* in who they are.

EATING AND TALKING

Remember how your mother used to say to you, "Don't talk with your mouth full . . ." Well, she was right, especially when it comes to eating and talking at parties. Some people have what is called *tongue-thrust swallow*, or *reverse swallow*. When they swallow, they stick their tongue out—the tongue protrudes outward as they swallow; it doesn't create a seal. The result can be very unaesthetic. Oftentimes you can see food on the person's tongue, which is obviously rather disgusting looking. If you have a problem with your swallow, you need to get some help from a licensed speech pathologist who is trained to handle your tongue thrust.

When you are eating at a party, by all means have a good time, and that means not feeling intimidated about what you eat and drink. If you are hungry, go ahead and eat. But under no circumstances are you to keep saying, "Oh, I shouldn't eat this . . . Oh, I shouldn't eat that . . ." to people around you. This does not put you in the best light.

Also, I can't stress enough how important it is to try not to talk and eat at the same time, no matter how excited or involved in the conversation you get. Now you might think, "Of course I would never talk with my mouth full." But you would be surprised at how many people do this without even being aware of it. Besides being unaesthetic, talking with a mouthful of food can be dangerous—life threatening. A friend of mine recently had to perform the Heimlich maneuver at a party where he was able to successfully dislodge a piece of meat that had become lodged in a guest's throat. So you really have to be careful when you are eating and socializing, otherwise it can result in a serious situation. When you're eating, in order to gracefully help keep a conversation going, you need to speak slowly, take your time, and only speak between bites—after you have swallowed. Your conversation is more important than the food. It is appropriate to take bites of food when you are listening or when there is a lull in the conversation. Therefore, expect slower responses during your conversation, which will give the other person time to taste and swallow their food.

NETWORKING AT PARTIES

Parties are a great place to network, but don't go to a party *just* to network.

Nobody likes or respects an obvious opportunist. I remember

being at a party once and meeting a young actress who said to me, "Who is your role model?" I began describing my attorney to her, who is one of the most beautiful, intelligent, sophisticated, and yet warm and loving women I have ever met in my life. She also has two gorgeous, intelligent, classy sons who are both in law school. After I told the girl this, she said to me, "Can you fix me up with one of her sons?" Her reaction was totally obnoxious. Instead of saying, "What a great lady. I would love to know somebody like her," all she could think of was that this was an opportunity for her to meet a guy—an intelligent future attorney from a well-connected family. This is a total turnoff, and doesn't put you in the best light.

When you meet people at parties, don't always think about what you can get from them, because it never works. If you really like a person, and you feel that you can help them out or that they can help you out, that's one thing, but don't fawn over people just because of what you think you can get out of them.

The point is that networking is a very positive thing, but first you need to get to know the person.

For example, I was once at a party and upon leaving a C.P.A. said to me, "By the way, if you ever need somebody to help you with your taxes or if I can answer any questions you might have with any of your tax problems, don't hesitate to give me a call." He wasn't pushy or obnoxious. Instead, he was open and communicative.

His motive in talking to me was not based on having me become his client; however, he did bring it up casually and unoffensively.

COMMUNICATING AT LARGE PARTIES

A lot of people hate large parties because they are overwhelmed by them. The larger the party, the more overwhelmed they become. If you feel yourself becoming overwhelmed at a party because there are just too many people and there is no way you can meet everyone you want to meet, just pick one person out at a time and go talk to them.

Get into the mood or the theme of the party and start approaching people, or groups of people. How do you approach a group engaged in conversation? First of all, you have to wait for a pause in the conversation. It is disconcerting if you interrupt a person. Someone could be telling a story and you could be stealing their limelight—a turnoff for them and the rest of the guests as well.

Whether you know everyone in the group or no one at all, feel free to approach the people in the group. When there is a lull in the conversation and you can relate to something that was said, don't hesitate to interject your comments. If nobody knows you, be sure to introduce yourself to the group after you say what you wanted to say.

For example, "By the way, I'm Carl Jones—a friend of Lisa."

When you want to exit a group of people and move onto another one, say that "It's been nice meeting you," or "Nice talking with you—please excuse me." Remember to keep smiling as you do this.

Sometimes the group you want to break into won't let you. They may be involved in a private or personal conversation and don't want to let anyone else in. You will usually get a sense that you are not welcome as the group will either ignore you—huddle close together to exclude you or blatantly inform you that they are engaged in a personal conversation.

If you, on the other hand, don't want anyone else to join your group or you want to have a private conversation with someone and another person tries to join the group, be honest with them but still be friendly. Say, "We're having a private conversation," or "We're discussing some personal business, but I would love to talk to you later." This way the person is allowed to save face and nobody goes away with hurt feelings.

If you are at a large party, it is also important not to shout. Unfortunately, too many people have a tendency to talk too loudly when there are a lot of people around, which can play havoc on your vocal cords. In order to gain more intimacy during communication, you just need to move closer to someone when you talk to them. You don't have to abuse your voice or sound obnoxious at large parties. All you have to do is get closer to people.

LIVENING UP A DULL PARTY

If you are a guest at a party where the people tend to be uptight and stuffy, you can unstuff them by *creating* little groups—by introducing yourself around to the people at the party, getting to know them, and even introducing them to one another. Make an effort to be talkative and open. Don't be afraid to go up to people and engage them in conversation.

On the other hand, there will be times when you can't liven up a dull party. Sometimes, the host or hostess will create the tone of the party by whom they invite and how they manage the party, so there will be nothing you can do about it.

If you find yourself around people who bore you—who aren't willing to open up and converse, or if you find that you are unable to "connect" with anybody—leave so that nobody sees that this experience has not brought out the best in you.

GOODBYES

A host needs to make every effort to make every guest feel that they are the most important guest at the party throughout the night. I have watched many socialites work a party, and the most successful of them make everybody they come in contact with feel like they are the best guest and most important person in the room. They consistently let their guests know how pleased they were that they could share the evening with them.

When your guests do leave, always walk them out, but before you do, ask them if they've had a good time and if there is anybody they would like to meet before they leave. If you feel that they should meet somebody, or they wish to meet someone before they leave, take this time to introduce them briefly. Be conscious of their time, because they already told you that they wanted to leave. You may want to say as you introduce them, "Mrs. Jones has to leave, but before she does I definitely want you to both meet one another."

What do you do with the rude guest who stays and stays and stays? How do you tell them to leave when you are ready to go to bed? Too many hosts and hostesses feel they are being rude if they ask a guest to leave. Even though the host is feeling exhausted, red-eyed, and nodding off, they will bear with it until the last guest leaves of their own accord. Don't be victimized by guests who overstay their welcome. As the host, you need to take charge. You don't have to be rude, but if someone is overstaying their welcome, you need to be direct, and once again, confront them—politely.

You might want to say, "John, I am so glad you came, and I don't mean to be rude, but I have to ask you to leave because I am so tired and I need to get some sleep. Let's get together later in the week when we can spend some more time with each other."

When you leave a party is up to you, but if you have to leave a party early, especially if it is a dinner party and you have just finished eating, let your host or hostess know ahead of time that you have another commitment and will have to leave early so that you don't appear to be rude.

Never leave a party unless you have said goodbye to your host. If you can't find them, or if they are engaged in heavy conversation, tell somebody close to the host that you have to leave and ask them to tell the host that you said goodbye. The next day, be sure to call the host to say how sorry you are about having to leave without saying goodbye.

Whenever you do leave a party, whether you are the first to leave or the last guest out the door, be sure to show your enthusiasm, especially if you had a good time. Don't be afraid to let your praises flow as you thank them for inviting you.

... 10 ...

Touchy Subjects

Touchy subjects have to be handled carefully. For example, how do you tell a person they've got bad breath? Well, Donald Trump was able to do it on the "Larry King Show." "Larry," he said, "do you mind if I sit back a little? Because your breath is very bad." Telling Larry King that he has bad breath on national television may not have been the most tactful thing to do. However, it may have been all that he could do to prevent Mr. King from invading Mr. Trumps's comfortable space.

If you need to tell someone their breath is off-putting, you may want to offer them a mint or let them know *in private*, in a caring, sensitive way. My friend Perry, who recently flew back from San Francisco, told me that he was forced to sit next to a man who smelled so bad that Perry's eyes started to water. Everybody within range of this gentleman had their air blowers on in this man's direction. Finally, Perry could take it no more. He ended up telling the stewardess that he was getting physically sick sitting next to this man, and he ended up getting moved up to the first-class section.

Perhaps this odiferous man was totally unaware of how much he offended people. If someone from the airline had been honest and direct with him, he may have made an attempt to ameliorate his problem. But the fact is, such confrontations are rare.

You don't have to blurt out, "Who died in here?" or "You smell like a dead rat," but you may want to say, "Sir, I don't mean to offend you, but your body odor is a bit strong and it would be in your best interest to take care of it so you don't offend others."

There are issues that practically everyone prefers to avoid; however, they need to be dealt with directly, honestly, and sensitively.

One of my clients has a friend whose dog has the worst case of bad breath. This woman adores her dog, and wants everyone else to, but every time my client would visit her friend, she could barely stand being in the same room with the poor animal.

Finally, she said, "Look, I love your dog, but there may be something wrong with his insides, because his breath doesn't smell normal. It may be something you want to have your vet look into."

My client was able to couch her criticism by expressing concern over her friend's pet rather than revulsion. As it turned out, the dog did end up having a gum disease. Had she been less sensitive and said, "Your dog's breath smells like he just swallowed a dead rat," that might have been the last she saw of the dog or her friend for a long time.

The main thing to remember is to allow the person to "save face," as the Japanese do. Use key phrases, such as: "Perhaps it would be in your best interest . . ." or "I don't mean to offend you, but . . ." or "I know this is a touchy subject, but . . ." and say it in private so that you don't embarrass the other person or yourself.

BEING THE BEARER OF BAD NEWS

When being the bearer of bad news—whether it means talking to someone about illness or death, reminding someone they owe you money, or telling someone that they are fired—you have to follow the golden rule: *Be as kind to others as you would have them be as kind to you.* If they were bearing your bad news, how would you want them to treat you? You wouldn't want them to say, "Your mother died," "Your dog just got killed," or

"Our relationship is over." The bearer of bad news can't be blunt or tactless. You have to be sensitive.

Sooner or later most of us will be put in the uncomfortable position of having to tell someone something that is going to possibly hurt them. Professional people—doctors and psychologists—are highly trained to do this. They tell the person in private, they touch the person, they allow the person to cry, even scream at them, to grieve. In being the bearer of bad news you may find yourself being yelled at, attacked verbally or even physically, or the person may start crying or become hysterical. If you are going to put yourself on the line, you need to be able to face the emotional consequences, and if you are concerned about the person's emotional stability, you need to have a professional counselor on hand.

Whether you are bearing bad news on a personal or professional level, you always need to be sensitive. When I was doing my post-doctorate work in medical genetics, where I saw patients with severe genetic diseases (deformities), I noticed that so many of my professors and the physicians were insensitive, cold, and distant toward these patients. It was a defense mechanism for breaking bad news to a parent whose child was born with a genetic defect.

There was, however, one professor, Dr. Robert J. Gorlin, a world-renowned geneticist and expert in the area of craniofacial abnormalities, who was the epitome of love, caring, and sensitivity. He was a man who exhibited compassion and warmth, and wasn't afraid to express himself physically by hugging and kissing a child born with facial deformities. His total acceptance of the child allowed the family to accept the child more readily. "Your baby has a genetic disorder that just happened. We don't know exactly why it happened. It just did. It wasn't something you did or caused. It's not your fault so it's nothing to feel guilty about. There is hope for your child. He'll require a lot of surgery throughout his life, but we have excellent surgeons who can help him. Hopefully he will be able to lead a productive life. You need to give him all the love and discipline you would with your other children, so just treat him like you would anyone else." Dr. Gorlin was also there to pick up the pieces when the family needed someone. He would be their shoulder to cry on, their wall to hit, as well as their source of understanding.

Men like Dr. Robert Gorlin need to be held up as examples of sensitive, caring, compassionate, loving, and understanding people whom we can all learn from.

INAPPROPRIATE CONVERSATIONS

What do you do if somebody brings up a subject that makes you feel very uncomfortable? You need to be direct and confront this person—even cutting them off mid-sentence. You may want to try phrases such as: "If you don't mind, I'd really rather not talk about that," or "I've had a terrible experience with that, I'd rather not re-stimulate it," or "I don't want to hear about . . ."

I have an adorable little Lhasa apso whom I love very much and whom I take with me practically everywhere I go. Inevitably, when I am out and about with him, there will be at least one insensitive person who will want to tell me a "dead dog" story. They will tell me how they once had a little dog. I will interrupt them immediately and say, "If it is a sad or negative story, I do not want to hear about it." I can't stand being exposed to people's stories about how their dog got an infection that went to its brain and it died, or how their dog was run over by a car and they found their smashed dog later that day. I refuse to hear these stories, and when I hear one coming I immediately cut it off—directly and abruptly.

Sometimes you may tell a person that you don't want to discuss a sensitive subject and they will ignore you and continue talking about it anyway. It is at that time that you have to take your breath in, hold it, bear down on your abdominal muscles, and say loudly: "THIS IS UNACCEPTABLE. I don't want to discuss this. Please respect my wishes as I respect yours."

Sometimes people will talk about things that they have no business bringing up with you—such as their love life, their sex life, their former lovers. Oftentimes hearing about these areas may make you feel extremely uncomfortable. You should tell them that the conversation is making you feel uncomfortable and that they may want to consider discussing this with someone else, perhaps a professional.

TALKING ABOUT YOUR ILLNESS

You don't want to have your health secrets spread around town. I was in a Seattle restaurant one weekend and there were two ladies sitting at a table next to me trying to outdo each other about who was the sicker of the two, with complaints about everything from the arthritis in their joints to the pains in their bowels. I felt like moving because I was disgusted with the subject matter of their conversation while I was eating and besides, I didn't want to catch anything from them.

Some people will discuss their physical problems with anyone who will listen in order to get pity, or perhaps just to have something to say. If someone is telling you their health problems, you need to tell them that you are sorry about their problems and you hope they get well, but perhaps they should save the details for their doctor. Most of the time these people are very lonely and unhappy, but you can't fall prey to the symptoms of their loneliness.

If you are ill, be very discriminating about whom you share your illness with, because it can come back to haunt you. For example, if you tell a friend that you have a case of herpes, you better be sure that the friend you tell doesn't tell a friend who tells a friend who tells a friend.

Not everybody can keep a secret, especially where relationships, health, or financial status are concerned.

TALKING ABOUT MONEY

The best way to lose a friend is to lend them money or to get involved with them financially. One of my clients was dating a man for only three months when he asked her to loan him $6,000 to help pay for his sick father's hospital bills. My client was so offended that she said, "What do I look like—the Bank of America?" It totally ended their relationship. She was so turned off by his asking her for money, which she didn't have to spare anyway, that she never went out with him again. My client was smart not to loan this man the $6,000. He turned out to be a gigolo.

In trying to help someone out whose friendship you value, you may find that they do not place the same value on your friendship as you do on theirs. Too many incidents have been described to me by clients throughout the years of a "friend" who has been negligent in paying back a loan.

If someone owes you money and has been delinquent in paying you back, you need to be direct and honest with them. For example, you need to say, "Six months ago I loaned you $100. I need it right now. When can I expect it?" Don't put them on the defensive, just confront them directly.

If they still don't pay you back, you need to step up your approach by telling them your relationship is in jeopardy, that you want them to pay you back by a certain date, and finally you need to tell them that this has caused you a great deal of hard feelings because you trusted them implicitly and feel taken advantage of.

Oftentimes, people keep these feelings in and harbor resentment when they don't need to. Once again, the direct and honest approach is the only thing that works.

TELLING SOMEONE THEY NEED COSMETIC ATTENTION

Perhaps one of the most difficult things to tell someone is that you think they need some cosmetic, dental, or facial work done. If you don't say it right, you are running the risk of the person telling you to mind your own business or never speaking to you again.

In my practice, as part of my professional responsibilities, I have often had to tell clients what I think they need to do in order to improve their "total image." After doing this for several years, I learned how never to offend anyone. If I see a patient whose teeth, for example, require cosmetic attention, the first thing I will do is ask them how they feel about the way their teeth look. If they say, "Fine," I will respect their feelings and not venture my opinion. However, if the person expresses concern about the appearance of their teeth or says, "Why do you ask?" I will be honest with them. I will, however, couch what I have to say with phrases such as "It's my professional opinion . . ." or "I think it would be in your best interest if . . ." or "There are so many safe and painless methods that are now available to make you look even better than you already look."

The key is to be positive—never making anyone feel ugly or defective, but telling them they can improve on what they already are. You may want to employ these techniques if you feel that someone close to you could use a nose job or dental rehabilitation or cosmetic surgery.

ASKING SOMEONE FOR A FAVOR

If you are going to ask somebody for a favor, make sure that (1) you know the person well; (2) that you can return the favor; and (3) that the favor is not the only reason you are befriending the person. Nobody likes to be used or taken advantage of.

Before you ask someone to do you a favor, make sure you at least know them. If a perfect stranger comes up to you at the airport, for example, and asks you to watch their bags for a moment, don't feel bad about saying, no, you can't be responsible for their belongings. This person obviously has a lot of nerve and little regard for your feelings. Watch out for your own feelings and don't let others impose themselves on you. You don't have to be rude. A firm "No, I'd rather not" is sufficient. Don't say "Yes" when you really don't want to be involved.

When you ask somebody for a favor, make sure it is not unreasonable and that you are not putting them under any pressure. For example, if a friend of yours is dating a movie director, you may be putting them on the spot by asking them if they will ask their boyfriend to get you a role in a movie.

Oftentimes, when somebody does you a favor, it is because of how they feel about you. Most of the time they don't want to do the favor, but they do it out of respect and love for you. If they are feeling uncomfortable, they may feel reluctant to do the favor for you, but they will do it anyway because they don't want to hurt your feelings. What you need to do is say, "This has nothing to do with our friendship, and I would greatly appreciate it if you could do me this favor. If you can't do it, or

152 · LILLIAN GLASS, PH.D.

if you feel in any way uncomfortable doing it, I completely understand," or you might say "We're friends enough for me to ask you this favor and, by the same token, we're friends enough that you can freely say no if you need to."

In asking someone for a favor, you need to, once again, let the person "save face," and allow them the opportunity to say "no" to your favor without taking offense at their reaction. Never ask them to agree to do the favor *before* you specify what it is.

Good communication requires that two people be honest and open with one another. So if you are going to ask somebody for a favor, (1) make sure it is a favor they can deliver without putting them on the spot; and (2) if they do say no because they don't feel comfortable about doing the favor for you, don't "cut them out of your life." Be sensitive to their needs as a friend, as well.

TELLING SOMEONE YOU'RE ON A DIET

Practically everyone I know has difficulty sticking to their diet. It is one of the most difficult things to do in our society, given all of the pressures to overeat. Under no circumstances should you tell someone that they need to go on a diet—it's none of your business. Nor is it your business to sabotage someone who is trying to diet.

Telling someone they need to go on a diet is the best way to lose a friend. There are people who will moan and groan about how fat they are. Let them moan and groan, but don't you start moaning and groaning along with them and tell them how fat they are and how much weight they need to lose. This has nothing to do with you. Somebody can tell you how fat they are, but if you start telling them how fat you think they are, they will inevitable become defensive and resentful.

How do you say "no" to people who push food on you when you are on a diet? What you need to do is look them right in the eye and say, "No, thank you, I am on a diet." If they persist, you can tell them, "I am under a doctor's treatment." If they still persist, maintain eye contact, keep silent for three seconds as you continue looking at them, take your breath in, hold it, then slowly and deliberately say "Noooo thank you. I told you I was on a diet." It's important for you to say this phrase slowly and deliberately in a projected tone.

You can also carry a card around with you like the one a doctor friend of mine in Beverly Hills gives to his patients. Dr. Howard Flak's card basically says, "My patient is on a strict diet. If you insist that my patient eat food that you suggest, please call my office and check with me first."

If somebody says "no" once to your offer of food, leave them alone. For some people who are trying to get their food intake under control, food is addictive. It's like putting a bag of cocaine in front of a cocaine addict, or a drink in front of an alcoholic. So if a person says no, *respect* them and leave them alone, because you may be feeding an addiction. They may say yes not to offend you, or eat just to shut you up. So please respect anyone on a diet.

Almost as bad as telling someone they need to go on a diet, there is another issue regarding weight that is a surefire turnoff. That is ranting and raving how good a person looks after they have lost weight and treating them with extreme enthusiasm when you hardly even talked to them before.

One of my clients, an attractive five-foot-eight-inch woman with a beautiful face, was fifty pounds overweight. When she lost the weight, men who hadn't noticed her before, and some who had been downright rude to her, started approaching her and being very friendly and seductive. She felt a lot of anger about this. Her thought was, How come they didn't speak as nicely to me when I was fat? She started becoming very hostile and downright nasty in her tone of voice when she spoke to these people. I assured her that this was not in her best interest, and although she didn't have to be rude or hostile, she needed to be honest about her feelings. In fact, she was able to tell one "interested" man whom she had known at work for several years that she really wanted nothing to do with him because he was rude to her when she was overweight.

Many people can relate to this *Why didn't they like me when I was fat* scenario. If you are feeling this way, you need to be direct and honest without putting the hostile edge in your tone.

If you notice that a person has lost a lot of weight and looks good, it's okay to tell them about how great they look; however, don't go on and on asking them about how much weight they lost and how they did it. This is really none of your business and can make for a lot of hard feelings and resentment.

SECRETS

We've talked about how you may not want to reveal all of your intimacies to even your best friend. Remember the saying: "Never tell your best friend anything you wouldn't want your worst enemy to know." There is a lot of truth to that, as we discussed. Oftentimes, secrets will turn against you.

A lot of children can certainly relate to this, because one of the most hurtful things children can do is tell secrets about one another. Unfortunately, telling secrets doesn't disappear when children grow up. Secret-telling continues right into adulthood in the form of gossip.

If you want to tell somebody a secret and you don't want it spread around, tell your therapist, your psychiatrist, or even your clergyman who has the vested responsibility to keep your secret a secret and not feed it into the local gossip mills. You can tell these people anything you want because in most cases they are professionally and legally bound not to break your confidences.

Clients will often tell me the most intimate secrets in confidence, and I will always keep secrets to myself. Anything my clients discuss with me never leaves the four walls of my office because of my professional obligation to them.

If there is something that you are not proud of or you simply do not want out in the open, don't tell *anyone* who is not professionally bound to keep it to themselves.

It is human nature to tell secrets because it oftentimes gives you an edge in a conversation. If you have information that nobody else has, it may be a form of one-upmanship. A lot of people tell secrets—not because they want to be malicious or mean but because they need to unload or unburden themselves. The secret may just be too much responsibility for them to carry around. So if you have a secret, tell your therapist or someone who you can be sure you can trust.

You can't stop anyone from telling a secret about you. But if someone is going to spread some gossip, especially about someone close to you, it may be in your best interest to cut them off by saying, "I really don't want to hear about it." You can also say, "Oh, I've heard those rumors before. They're just rumors."

Doing this can stop the gossip from spreading.

SAYING NO TO DRUGS AND ALCOHOL

There are a lot of campaigns combatting drugs and alcohol: "Say No to Drugs," or "Say No to Alcohol." These are wonderful, well-meaning campaigns; however, when it comes right down to the actual situation, for many it may not be that easy to say no to someone trying to push that drink, that line of cocaine, or that hit of marijuana on you, while they're saying, "All your friends are doing it." It takes a lot of personal strength to say "no" to someone and really mean it. In order to help fortify your strength, you need to maintain direct eye contact, pause in silence for three seconds as you continue to look at the person, take in your breath, and hold it. Firmly say, "No, thank you. I'd rather not"—all the time maintaining your eye contact and being in control of your breathing. Oftentimes, just being in control of your breathing can help you be in control of other things you have to confront.

If the people around you persist and make light of your response, saying, "Oh, come on—go ahead—it won't hurt you," or "Come on, have a drink and relax," or "This will help you feel better," keep maintaining eye contact and control over your breathing. Say as you draw out your tone, "I told you I didn't want a drink (or drugs)—thank you anyway." If they persist—LEAVE. This is not a friend. This is a person who obviously doesn't respect you or what you have to say. By leaving, you are respecting yourself.

You may say, "Yes, but what about peer pressure—what if everyone else *is* doing it? I'll feel left out." My answer is get a new set of peers or new friends. It doesn't really matter what anyone who does drugs or drinks excessively "thinks" about you because they can't think straight anyway. We've all heard the expression "If you lie down with dirty dogs you'll get fleas." If you want to live a life where you are in control of all your senses and you see the world clearly and not distorted by drugs and alcohol, you need to be around people who are like that, too. You need to get rid of all the people who are negatively influencing you. Instead, find people who encourage a healthy, positive life-style.

WHAT TO SAY IN THOSE EMBARRASSING MOMENTS

What do you say when you walk into an important business meeting and your shoulder pads fall out on the floor from under your dress? What do you do when you've invited that new special person over for the very first time only to find your dog coming to join the two of you with your bra hanging out of his mouth? What do you do when you go out for that important lunch meeting and you spill water all over everyone? Or worse, you drop food all over your nice white shirt? You LAUGH! If you make light of the situation, so will everyone else around you. On the other hand, if you fumble around and become disheveled and disoriented or angry and hostile, you'll make everyone else around you feel uncomfortable. In order to regain your composure, use the Tension Blow-Out exercise and then make light of what happened so that you set the tone for everyone else around you.

PEOPLE WHO WANT TO MIND YOUR BUSINESS

There are people who for whatever reason are nosybodies. They get their kicks out of minding your business. They want to know the who, what, when, where, how, and whys of your life. These intrusive people need to be set straight right away. When you encounter someone who is asking questions beyond your comfort zone, you need to put a stop to it immediately. You don't have to put the person on the defensive and say "None of your business." Instead, you can use phrases like "It's not something I'd like to discuss at the present time," "I feel uncomfortable discussing this topic with you," "It's not appropriate for me to discuss it with you," or "I'd rather not talk about it with you."

If they continue to persist, you may want to say, "I feel you're overstepping your bounds," or "I'll discuss it with you when I feel it's a better time for me." This way you are setting limits and keeping your comfort zone safe. By saying this you are in control and you do not fall prey to the nosybodies' curiosity.

SEXUAL AND RACIAL SLURS

When a person makes a sexist comment or a racial slur, it really tells you a great deal about that person. It may reflect the person's true feelings or prejudices. Whether it is intentional or not, anybody who makes a sexist or racial slur is running the risk of alienating anyone who hears it.

It may also reflect their narrow or small-mindedness, insecurities, or inflexibilities. If you hear a person making such a comment, it may not be your place to correct them or to admonish them unless you know them well enough to do so. The only exception to this is when the slur or pejorative comment is directed toward you. In that case, it's appropriate to address the offensive remark immediately.

One of my clients—a black, Harvard-educated attorney—was negotiating with a studio executive over the telephone. They had never met one another but developed a warm and friendly telephone relationship. One day the executive made a pejorative comment about blacks. My client immediately interjected, "Well, I'm black and I don't appreciate what you said." That put an end to the negotiation process.

In this day and age there is absolutely no room for racial prejudices of any kind. As we enter the Communications Age where people from all walks of life and all ethnic backgrounds are being exposed to one another more and more, racial and sexist comments will only serve to ostracize and alienate the person making the comments.

CATCHING SOMEONE IN A LIE

People lie for different reasons—to "save face" or to impress others. Some lie to *not* hurt others. Often, people who lie don't even look at it as lying but merely stretching the truth or exaggerating what is. No matter how you look at it, catching someone in a lie no matter how big or small is embarrassing and can even destroy trust in a relationship.

What do you do if you catch someone in a lie? It depends what kind of lie it is—if it's an exaggeration or told for the sake of impressing someone, it really doesn't matter. You generally don't want to expose that person and cause them embarrassment. However, if a person is lying to take advantage of a situation, you need to expose that person immediately by confronting them openly with the truth. Instead of accusing them of lying, you need to say something like "I feel that there is a difference of opinion here" or "My facts seem to be different than yours" or "I disagree with you."

... 11 ...

The Right Words for Special People

There are a number of people and situations you will encounter throughout your life that will require special communications skills. You may encounter people whom you may not ordinarily come in contact with like children, teenagers, the elderly, celebrities, people from different cultures, or the disabled—even the terminally ill. You may even have to speak to people with whom you have never felt comfortable around, like your doctor, lawyer, or C.P.A., as well as other difficult people in difficult situations.

TALKING TO CHILDREN

Talking to children often begins as early as the fetus is in the womb and has even been termed "fetal communication."

Researchers have known for years the importance of early stimulation in regard to communication, but now studies have found that communication may be important before birth.

Because all of the sensory systems are essentially developed by the time a fetus is seventeen to twenty-four weeks old, it may be feasible to communicate with a developing fetus. In fact, studies have shown that fetuses can respond to bright-colored lights—that they calm down when they hear classical music, and that they become aroused and develop an elevated heartbeat in utero whenever they hear rock music regularly. In fact, sonogram studies—in which one can see the outline of a fetus in utero—have shown that the child moves around more in the presence of loud noises.

There are several pre-natal specialists like Dr. Rene Van de Carr of Hayward, California, who believe that talking to a child in utero can increase verbal development, which he verified in a study of 150 mothers. He encourages mothers to use a paper megaphone and repeat certain words and phrases.

Birth consultants, such as Binnie Dansby or Terri Belfroy of Los Angeles, actually teach parents how to talk to their children in utero by using calming tones and repetitive words and phrases. Birth consultants have discovered this creates more alert babies, which can have a greater impact on early speech and language development. When the child is born, early infant interaction—talking to the child—creates stronger bonding between parent and child that can further stimulate speech and language development and open up communication early on.

In communicating with children, you, of course, need to set limits through your vocal tone, but calm and firm explanations have been shown to achieve more long-lasting, consistent, positive results than erratic, hostile commands. The bottom line in communicating with your child is to encourage self-respect and self-esteem. Children need to be encouraged to talk about their feelings and express emotion so they don't react negatively throughout life. Most of all they need to be treated like people. Parents who are of the philosophy that children should be seen and not heard, or who say "Be quiet," or "ignore" a child who asks them a question, are creating more damage to their child's self-esteem than they realize.

You need to *always* answer the child—make them feel that what they have to say is important. Even if you are bombarded by constant questions or are too busy at the moment, tell them you will talk to them later. Then *don't* forget to talk to them later. Respecting a child's communication fosters self-esteem throughout the child's life.

In communicating with children, the first rule is "Baby talk is out." A child's speech structures aren't as fully developed so mis-pronunciations often occur. Although this is normal, it shouldn't be re-stimulated. In fact, the adult should repeat to the child how to correctly pronounce words and phrases so that they instill good models for speech and language development.

The same is true for encouraging proper language development. Even if a child says, "Me go," which is normal for a toddler's development, by saying it correctly and teaching the child to repeat it after you, you will be fostering proper language development. It doesn't even matter if the child can't repeat what you said as long as they can hear it from you correctly on a *consistent* basis. They will be learning the proper way of saying it as they receptively learn the language.

TALKING TO FOREIGNERS

Many people feel uncomfortable when they have to speak to a person from a foreign country. Unfortunately, too many people are so busy looking at the differences between people that they neglect to realize how alike we all are—no matter where we come from or where we live. There are obvious language differences, but real communication between people—no matter what their background is—comes from the *heart!*

As human beings we have more similarities than differences: We all feel, we all love, we all hurt, we all cry, we all feel joy! These feelings are what allow us, regardless of culture, to communicate with one another. Constant awareness of this can totally abolish the ignorant and ugly prejudices we may harbor against people who are different from us.

"Warmth" manifested by openness, honesty, and a genuine smile and respect for the other person is the universal language that can bridge any cultural gap.

If you are "warm" and open, it is easy to speak to anyone from a foreign country. Ask questions about life-styles in their country—where they live, how they grew up, what their business is like, what their homelife is like, what's important to them, what means the most to them in their life, what things they would like most to change about their life, what they are most proud of, what they'd like to do most in life, what things they find easy to adapt to in our culture, what things they find difficult to adapt to. You will be surprised at how much you'll learn from the answers to these questions—not only about them but about yourself as you compare your life to theirs.

Recently I met a Russian film director. In talking with him, I felt like I was in a movie. While listening to the visual images he described, I kept fantasizing about my life and his life and how different they were, yet how alike we were. I felt his anguish when he mentioned how difficult it was to learn English when he first arrived here and how difficult it was to get started. I felt his excitement in finally being successful in a new country after years and years of hard work and dedication. Even though we were culturally different, I could definitely relate to him through our common bond of being dedicated and working hard.

In my practice, I meet a lot of people who want to reduce their foreign accents. I recently met a man from Singapore who told me the most wonderful things about how clean his city is. He said it was so gorgeous and described everything in great detail. When I ended up going to Singapore I recalled much of what this man had told me. It gave me greater insight into the people and the culture.

If you want to talk to someone but don't understand their language, you can use gestures or try to figure out what they're saying from words common to so many of the Romance languages. It is also an excellent idea to study tapes of a language so you know basic words and phrases and can get along. This came in very handy when I went to Italy and met a basso profondo opera star who didn't speak a word of English and I didn't speak a work of Italian. We were seated next to one another in the same compartment for two hours on a train from Rome to Florence. Between the gestures, facial expressions, my knowledge of Spanish, and the significant phrases I learned from my language tapes, we had a wonderful two-hour conversation.

Most people feel embarrassed to try to speak with a foreigner. Even if you only know a few words or phrases—gesture, talk, communicate! It doesn't matter if your grammar is not correct or that your pronunciation is poor. As long as you try, you will endear people to you.

COMMUNICATION CUSTOMS OF VARIOUS CULTURES

Even though "warmth" is the key element in narrowing the communications gap between foreigners, there are some basic rules to help avoid misunderstandings (faux pas) depending on the specific country.

This section is designed to help you learn about communication customs in various parts of the world.

ATTITUDE, GESTURES AND BODY LANGUAGE

AFRICA	• Warm, friendly, hospitable communication
	• Personal space between members of same sex is closer than in United States
	• In certain tribes, winking means you want a child to leave the room
AUSTRALIA	• Avoid overt signs of familiarity
	• Hugging
	• Yawning = rude
	• Thumb-hitching sign = vulgar
AUSTRIA	• Quiet and orderly in public
	• Talking with hands in pocket is considered rude
	• Gum chewing is considered rude
	• Legs not to be rested on desk
BELGIUM	• Arm-pumping handshake
	• Casualness = rude
	• Gum chewing = rude
	• Hands in pockets = rude

- Good posture expected
- Pointing finger = rude
- Putting feet on chair = rude

BRITISH ISLES
- More reserved
- Avoid excessive warmth in conversation
- Overt friendliness and overt gestures not accepted
- Backslapping and arms around someone = rude
- Leg crossing only when one knee is over the other; otherwise = rude
- Shouting = offensive

CANADA/UNITED STATES
- Eye contact
- Open friendliness
- Open displays of affection accepted

CENTRAL AMERICA
- Yawning, stretching, and putting hands in pocket while talking = rude
- Emotion in speech

CHINA/TAIWAN/HONG KONG
- Hospitable
- Reserved modesty
- Don't use enthusiastic approval
- Touching and gesturing not part of communication pattern
- Smiling expresses affection
- Winking is rude as is eye blinking at someone
- Point palm and fingers down to beckon someone (reverse of American gesture)

- Pointing done by extending open hand
- Same sex hand in hand acceptable
- Denies praise when complimented

FIJI
- Touching while talking

FRANCE
- Firm, pumping-arm handshake = rude
- Very punctual
- American "o.k." sign means "zero"
- French "o.k." sign = thumbs up
- Snapping fingers of both hands = vulgar
- Never sit with legs apart—cross legs with one knee over the other
- Talking with hands in pocket = rude
- Gum chewing = rude
- Yawning and scratching = rude

GREECE
- No = upward nod of head (like American yes)
- Yes—tilting head from side to side
- Lateness is common
- Emotion in speech

HUNGARY/ROMANIA/ BULGARIA/POLAND/ CZECHOSLOVAKIA
- Formal, reserved
- Gestures are similar to American except in Bulgaria where gestures for yes and no are opposite of American gestures

INDIA
- No public displays of affection
- Use chin to point instead of fingers
- Will ask permission before leaving to say goodbye to express humility and respect
- Showing soles of feet = rude.

ISRAEL
- Open communication
- Readily communicate opinion and points of view
- Informality and directness
- Emotionally expressive

ITALY
- People of the same sex often walk arm in arm
- Yawning = rude
- Gesture with one hand to express points
- Two-hand gesture = rude and inappropriate

JAPAN
- Impolite to chew gum
- Don't use many hand gestures
- Sit erect with both feet on floor when you speak
- Laughing may not only be a sign of humor but of distress or embarrassment, or feeling uncomfortable
- Respect/honor—self-dignity important character traits

KOREA
- Feet not to be used to move objects
- Hitting fist into cupped hand = vulgar
- Never use finger to beckon; use entire hand with palm down

- Slight bow when entering and leaving
- or passing a group of people = respectful
- No overt displays of affection
- Standing with hands in pocket or on hips = defiance
- Yawning = rude

MIDDLE EAST
- Never use left hand
- Emotionally expressive
- Formal and proud

NEW ZEALAND
- Waving is fine to recognize someone
- Gum chewing and yawning = rude

PORTUGAL
- Conservative
- Reserved in gestures; avoid overly physical gestures
- To beckon someone, extend arm, palm down, and wave fingers back and forth

SINGAPORE
- Great respect paid to elderly
- Touching someone's head impolite
- In crossing legs, one's knees are placed directly over other knee—foot should never be pointed at anyone

SOUTH AMERICA
- Smiling and a good word for strangers considered sociable
- Politeness and hospitality proper etiquette
- Maintaining eye contact when talking = important
- Excessive hand gestures = rude

- Moving feet unconsciously while sitting down = rude
- Drooping posture = disrespectful
- Crossed legs are o.k. unless ankle is on knee for men
- Leg crossing for women = unladylike

SOVIET UNION
- Approval = thumbs-up sign
- Never use American o.k. sign = vulgar
- Sitting with ankle crossed on knee = offensive
- Express emotion when speaking

SPAIN
- Warm and friendly communication
- Project social position and elegance
- Image conscious

SWITZERLAND
- O.K. to cross legs—stretching legs out = rude
- Hands in pocket when talking = rude
- Waving to someone across street is acceptable
- Not waving = rude

THAILAND
- Never touch person's head or pass object over it
- Never point bottoms of feet in direction of another or move objects with feet
- Placing arm over back of chair = rude
- No public display of affection
- Same-sex friends hold hands

ACCENTS AND DIALECTS

Why do most of us mimic someone when we hear an accent and a dialect? We will often start to talk like them, which we then feel embarrassed about.

Oftentimes, Americans will hear a British person or Southerner and find that they are unconsciously copying an upward lilt or a drawn-out tone. There is nothing wrong with this so don't be embarrassed. Most of us do this when we want to identify or relate to another person—to either make them feel more comfortable with us, or vice versa. In most instances, the person you are talking to won't even notice what you are doing, but if they do, they most likely will be flattered.

I adore accents and dialects and have been pleased to be able to reproduce them. In fact, a large part of my private practice involves teaching stars how to gain accents for different movie roles—Rob Lowe, a Southern accent for *Square Dance*, and French and Spanish accents in *Bad Influence*; Tristan Rogers, a Russian and Irish accent; Mickey Rourke, a New Orleans accent with a cleft palate, to name a few.

I've worked with actors to help them lose or modify an accent—singer Julio Iglesias to modify his Spanish accent to sing for "All the Girls"; Dolph Lundgren *(Rocky IV)* to lose his Swedish accent; Christopher Lambert to lose his French accent; Ben Vereen to lose a black accent; and singer Sheena Easton to lose a Scottish accent for her American acting roles.

Anyone can learn to change or modify their accent. Many people are terribly self-conscious about their accent or dialect, which may cause them considerable embarrassment. I've had people come to me with accents who were so self-conscious about them that they felt that it limited every aspect of their lives.

Others have come to me with tales of how frustrated they were that nobody understood them. In these cases, I would usually encourage the person to change their accent. However, if a person feels comfortable with their accent and the way they sound, I encourage them to keep their accent. I feel that accents add charm and character to a person.

Unfortunately, there are people who react to others' accents with prejudices and ugliness. This happened to an Iranian businessman client of mine who did very well in the United States before the political climate in his country changed. Afterwards, he found that his Farsi dialect became more of a hindrance in business so he attempted to modify his accent. When he succeeded, he noticed that his business succeeded as well.

In cases where a person's accent hinders their advancement socially and professionally, I strongly encourage accent reduction. A forty-year-old computer analyst who worked for a major company had a thick Chinese accent, which kept him from being promoted—according to this boss. He was a brilliant man who was educated in the United States. He felt that as long as he understood and could speak English he was fine. What he didn't realize was that not everyone was pleased with his ability to communicate in English. In fact, most of the time nobody could understand his rapid, clipped, mispronounced speech. By improving his accent, he received a higher paying job and found that his co-workers were friendlier to him. He even had an added bonus of being invited to co-workers' homes to socialize—something that had never happened before. Now they could actually carry on a conversation with him and actually understand him.

Most people do not harbor prejudices because a person has an accent but because they are frustrated that they cannot understand a person with an accent. So if you find people saying, "What?" or "Huh?" or "Excuse me?" or "Can you repeat that?" you may want to think about getting help to eliminate or modify your foreign accent.

TALKING TO CELEBRITIES

Many celebrities appreciate being noticed and acknowledged— otherwise they wouldn't be in the public eye. Most celebrities will appreciate your recognition of them, but *how* you recognize them makes a difference. Never interrupt them when they are eating or busily engaged in a conversation.

When you do get the courage to speak to them—remember that they are just like anyone else only they have more publicity than other people do. Don't be afraid to say hello and to say something positive or find a common bond. For example, if you're from Chicago and meet a celebrity from the same town— tell them. If you have a friend in common or you have visited a place they just came back from, they'll often appreciate your attempts to find a common bond and will usually respond positively. Just remember to treat them with respect and kindness and be considerate of their time. If you want an autograph, ask for one, but don't get carried away and give them a list of all your relatives to sign autographs for. Sometimes you may ask for an autograph and you will be refused. Don't take this personally and stop watching their movies or going to their concerts. Often, if a celebrity signs one autograph they will be deluged by other autograph seekers in a matter of moments. I've seen this with my own eyes. It can be quite disturbing if the celebrity is in a hurry or has other issues on their mind.

Most of the time celebrities love the attention, but because of security reasons—mentally unstable fans—most celebrities are very cautious in this day and age. Don't lunge toward them, scream, or faint when you do come into contact with them. Only shake their hand if they extend it first.

COMMUNICATING WITH THE DISABLED

No matter how disabled a person is—whether they are blind, deaf, deformed, or paralyzed—treat them with the dignity and respect they deserve as a human being.

Remember the words in the movie *Elephant Man:* "I am not an animal—I am a man." John Merrick was saying that even though he was different, he was still a human being deserving of all the respect accorded to him as a human by another human being.

All too often people unknowingly are insensitive and downright cruel to disabled people because they don't know how to talk to them. This can be frustrating to both the disabled and non-disabled as well.

One of my dearest friends is Kirk Kilgour, who is severely disabled and paralyzed from the neck down. He was an Olympic volleyball champion and international volleyball star before an accident injured his spine. This gorgeous six-foot-four strapping man is now confined to a wheelchair. At first you may say, "Oh, how pitiful, how sad," but there's nothing to be sad about because Kirk has made the best of his life. He's now a sportscaster for ABC, Prime Ticket, Turner Broadcasting, and the Sports Channel. He is one of the most sensuous, expressive, classy gentlemen one could hope to meet. After spending a few moments talking to Kirk, most people tend to forget about the wheelchair or anything related to his disability because Kirk has the ability to make those around him feel very comfortable. That stems from a comfort about who he is as a person.

I've learned a lot about communicating with people who have handicaps from Kirk's openness and directness. Too often people don't know how to talk to a disabled person. They try to ignore the fact that the person has a disability because they feel so uncomfortable themselves. It's understandable—since most people haven't been exposed to those with severe disabilities.

Kirk and other disabled people I've worked with appreciate it when people directly ask them about themselves—like children tend to do. A child is often very curious, and innocently and freely asks questions like "What happened to you? How do you put on your clothes? How do you eat? How do you brush your teeth?" Being as direct as children are can often break the ice and allow you to get to know the disabled person as you directly and openly confront their disability.

Many people feel awkward when greeting a disabled person. For example, it's an automatic response to reach out to shake someone's hand. However, when someone is paralyzed from the neck down and has no use of their arms and hands, it can often embarrass the non-disabled person. Most disabled people, like Kirk, will try to make it easier on the non-disabled person by telling them what to do.

When a person reaches out to shake Kirk's hand, he immediately interjects, "Just grab my arm and squeeze." This openness allows for a more cohesive bond between the two.

When talking to a disabled person, especially one you've just met, treat them with the same dignity and respect you would a non-disabled person. For example, if you want to discuss an intimate detail in the life of a disabled person, simply follow the same guidelines you would use when speaking to any and all people.

When talking to a disabled person, try not to ask question upon question. This happens all too often when people are feeling uncomfortable or nervous around someone. Ask a question and then let them answer. Permit them time to ask you a question so that they can get to know you as well. Let them finish speaking before you go on to the next question or topic.

If you ask a disabled person a question that they may not want to answer, they will usually tell you that they don't want to talk about it. In that case, apologize and be gracious. However, in most cases, the majority of disabled people will want to tell you things about themselves. They will want to share with you and will usually appreciate your directness and your interest in them. Disabled people have been in the unique position of explaining their disabilities and their differences so often that they are used to all the attention.

Sometimes, the attention they receive from others may be heartbreaking. I remember a devastating incident that happened to a "little person," whom I met while I was doing my post-doctorate training in medical genetics at Harbor UCLA Medical Center. I escorted this lovely woman into an examining room. As we walked through the hallway, a young girl of normal height pointed at this woman and started laughing and giggling at her. I was appalled and went over to this little girl and said, "You shouldn't laugh at this woman. It's not nice— she is just like you only she's smaller."

The "little person" interrupted me, took my hand, and with a calm smile said, "Oh, Dr. Glass, don't bother. I'm used to that. I get that all the time."

It broke my heart. This woman should not *have* to be used to ugliness and ridicule as she walks into a room. We need to treat and talk to the disabled just like we talk to anyone else— with the dignity and respect all human beings deserve.

TALKING TO THE BLIND

While I was in my post-doctoral training a doctor, who should have known better, was talking to a blind patient in a very loud voice—literally shouting at the patient as he asked him about his medical history. Finally, the blind man just shook his head and laughed. "Doctor," he said, "I'm not deaf, I'm blind, so please stop yelling at me."

Because blind people don't have facial cues and feedback to know when to continue and when to stop talking, they will have a tendency to keep talking, not knowing when to stop. Don't be afraid to touch them as you interrupt them to let them know that you want to say something.

You have to help blind people out and let them know when it's appropriate to keep talking and when it's appropriate to stop talking. So many blind people are very articulate and verbal that oftentimes you may start nodding your head in agreement with what they are saying but that feedback doesn't work. You need to verbalize "yes," "no," or "I understand," in order to provide feedback. This happened to me as I met a blind speech pathologist in Austria—a logopedist. I was so thoroughly impressed with what he had to say that I found myself forgetting he was blind and I was nodding my head. So be sure to be as verbal with them as often as possible. I might also add that when you walk with a blind person, lead the way, keeping their hand on top of yours, and walking and talking slowly and steadily. Don't drag them.

TALKING TO THE DEAF

Deaf people require special consideration when you talk to them. Oftentimes you need to (1) speak more slowly; (2) speak louder (if they are hard of hearing); (3) open your mouth wider and articulate so that a deaf person can understand you; (4) put a lot of emotion in your speech and use facial animation so that the emotion can be determined by your facial expression; and (5) make sure that you are facing a deaf person directly— otherwise they cannot read your lips.

If you do not understand something a deaf person says, maintain eye contact with them, touch their arm, and ask them to slow down. They need to do the same to you if they don't understand you.

I've worked with hundreds of deaf clients, and the reason I've had success in helping them improve their communication skills is because I treat them as though they are hearing enabled—actually they have normal bodies and speech mechanisms. The only difference is that their speaking muscles may be weaker and they can't hear themselves so I teach them how to feel themselves talk.

I usually will treat them as I would any other client who has a foreign accent and the results are remarkable. One of my clients, Eva Jo, a thirty-eight-year-old computer technologist, never spoke in her life, and now she can be understood. Her boss can understand her, and for the very first time in her life her family can carry on a conversation with her without using sign language.

My work with Marlee Matlin culminated at the 1988 Academy-Awards ceremony when she spoke for the very first time. It was perhaps the most dramatic example of listening to a deaf person speak perfectly after undergoing extensive speech therapy.

By instilling confidence in her and treating her like a hearing person (employing the five steps mentioned above), and by helping her to train and strengthen her throat, tongue, and facial muscles to make sounds—along with teaching her to control her breathing and pitch level—she was literally able to make history when she spoke.

Sometimes my deaf clients speak so well, I'll forget they are deaf and call their name when their backs are turned. I'm not the only one who forgets. Producer Samuel Goldwyn was so impressed with Marlee Matlin's speaking ability after having a lively and animated discussion with her that he whispered in her ear at the end of the meeting. Even though she cannot hear whispers, the fact that Mr. Goldwyn forgot she was deaf was a tribute to Marlee's abilities as a communicator.

TALKING TO PEOPLE WITH SPEECH PROBLEMS

According to the American Speech, Language, and Hearing Association, over 22 million Americans are afflicted with some type of speech and communication disorder. My feeling is that it is one out of every two people because I include such annoying speech habits among speech disorders—interrupting, using too high a pitch, talking too rapidly, mumbling, sounding too nasal, using "like," "um," and other similar filler words, mispronunciation, speaking too loudly, and speaking too softly.

So it is inevitable that at one time or another, either socially or in doing business, you will be communicating with somebody who has some type of speech problem.

STUTTERERS

One of the most common speech problems that can severely impair a person's communication is stuttering. There are many theories as to what stuttering is, why stuttering began, and what type of people stutter. The bottom line is that it is a disorder that can impair a person's ability to communicate. It can affect their life and their self-esteem and their ability to relate their needs to you. It can even affect your ability to communicate with them.

The first rule in dealing with someone who stutters is never finish a sentence for them. Second, never give them armchair speech therapy. Most stutterers have heard it all and are undergoing therapy or have had some type of treatment already. Third, never tell them to slow down, relax, or take it easy, even though you mean well. This is not only very embarrassing, but may make them more self-conscious. Fourth, maintain face contact with the stutterer no matter how uncomfortable it is for you.

Stuttering is defined as a repetition, a hesitation, or a block on a word. In essence, all of us have stuttered at some time or another. We all stutter in front of different people. Sometimes we're in front of a boss who makes us feel intimidated and we may stutter, or we may be playing the *I think that you think that I think* game and stutter in front of someone we've just met. On the other hand we just may have a word that triggers stuttering behavior. Whenever we talk about a certain topic that makes us nervous, many of us stutter. So stuttering happens to all of us when our minds work so much faster than our mouths. We think so much more rapidly than we speak, so the trick is to coordinate the neuro-motor function of our mouths in order to connect our thoughts with the mechanics of sound production and establish meaningful words and communication. In order for this to happen, we need desperately to be in control of our speech mechanism. This can only be achieved through learning to coordinate vocal flow, muscles, breathing, and coordinating our breathing and our talking.

Because almost all of us have experienced stuttering, we can all be sensitive to how people who stutter feel.

Everyone's heart in America went out to football hero Lester Hayes as they watched him being interviewed by Bryant Gumbel after winning the Superbowl pass. Bryant held the microphone for what seemed to be an eternity in front of Lester while Lester's lips moved automatically in a convulsive manner and his tongue protruded, his eyes blinked, and no sound came out. It was perhaps the most humiliating experience in Lester's career and reflected everyone's worst nightmare. Now we can understand why the fear of speaking in front of people is one of the greatest fears most people have.

As a result of this tragedy, which cost Lester millions of dollars in commercial endorsements, Lester took charge of his speech problem and began working with me to combat his stuttering. Today he is a well-respected public speaker and has his stuttering under control as he gives motivational speeches across the country.

APHASICS

Aphasia is the impaired ability to communicate due to brain damage from a stroke or trauma. The person may have difficulty speaking, they may have memory loss and/or word loss, and they may not be able to understand what you're saying or express what they want to say.

This is one of the most frustrating speech problems, and requires a great deal of patience. It's frustrating for both the person with aphasia and the person trying to talk to an aphasic who was once a viable, vibrant speaker and no longer is. Patience is the key along with not treating the person like a child. Allow them to maintain their dignity and respect above all. Keep constant eye contact/face contact and don't be afraid to touch them. Speak slowly and in short, complete sentences. Consult with the patient's speech and language pathologist so they can help you incorporate their techniques at home or whenever you are around the person who has aphasia or is brain-damaged.

TALKING TO PEOPLE WITH ANNOYING SPEECH HABITS

I'm often asked what to do if the way someone speaks annoys you. For example, what do you say to a woman you're dating who has an annoying lateral lisp, which annoys you so much that you're thinking of breaking up with her?

Well before you "throw the baby out with the bath water," and end a good relationship because of an annoying habit, you need to confront her.

In a kind, gentle manner you must first ask her how she feels about her lisp. If she is defensive or likes it, still tell her your feelings, and if she doesn't want to do anything about it, you may be doing her the best favor by bringing it to her attention.

By bringing her lisp to her attention, you may even improve how people perceive her and in turn improve the quality of her lot in life.

Lisping is cute as a child, but studies show that adults who lisp are perceived as being less intelligent, not trustworthy, and less attractive than those who don't lisp.

Several people I know who heard a mayoral candidate with a severe lisp on television called me to tell me how shocked they were that a man in public office could allow himself to be in the public eye without taking care of his lisp. Perhaps it was his lisp and poor total image that contributed to his losing his mayoral bid.

Lisping is fixable; usually it's due to improper tongue placement. The tongue tip needs to be pressing in back of the lower four teeth to produce a proper "s" and "z" sound.

If someone you care about has any other type of annoying speech problem like a raspy voice or a nasal tone, a high-pitched voice, or keeps saying "like," or "um," or "you know" all the time, you owe it to them, as a concerned friend, to bring it to their attention, but in a loving, positive, upbeat way in which you offer them alternatives. Don't just say, "You sound awful"—tell them that you know that they may feel sensitive about their speech. Bring it up with sensitivity and love in order not to hurt them. You can even offer a book or audiotape such as *Talk to Win*, to help them, give the name of a qualified speech pathologist, or tell them to write or call the American Speech, Language, and Hearing Association in Rockville, Maryland, where they can locate a qualified professional in their area.

... 12 ...

The Right Words for Special Encounters

TALKING TO PEOPLE WHO ARE TERMINALLY ILL

Talking to people who are terminally ill is perhaps one of the most difficult things in the world to do. With the advent of AIDS, too many people have watched someone close to them die an untimely death.

Perhaps we can use the example of a certain African national group that gathers the entire family and village together around the person who is going to die. Everyone in the village takes turns rubbing the person and massaging him or her. They cuddle, hug, and hold the person. They laugh with them and cry with the dying person. They are totally there for that person until that person is at peace and passes on. This is a beautiful way of communicating with someone who is dying—to be available and treat those who don't have many days left on the earth with all the love and respect and kindness and attention you have to give.

Perhaps the modern-day version of this kind of love is the Wellness Community that Gilda Radner talked about in her book *It's Always Something* (1989) before she died of ovarian cancer.

Oftentimes people who are dying inspire us to tell the truth—

to say things we wish we had said to them earlier. We need to always say what we mean and not be afraid to express love, because a good word, a kind phrase, an honest, sincere, lovely thought is worth more than a million dollars. Never be afraid to share your thoughts and feelings with people you care about.

One of my clients, Ralph, a fifty-two-year-old man, was a chain smoker and developed throat cancer. As a result of the radiation therapy he came to see me to help him regain his voice. Usually patients who have the cancer and the extent of damage he had do not survive long. I knew this when he began treatment, but I made each day, each session, a joyous occasion. We would laugh and gossip and talk, and I would tell him stories and we would really have a good time. I would ask him his opinion of things, which made him feel worthwhile.

When he finally died I got the most beautiful call from his best friend, his wife, and his many family members who said that I touched his life. The most heart-warming call I received, which made me see what a difference love and kindness can make in someone's life no matter how long they have left on earth, was from his best friend who said, "Ralph only had six months to live, but he felt blessed that you were part of those six months. You made each and every day of his life worth living. He really loved you."

If it's a person's last days, make them laugh, touch them, hold them, and make them feel like a "person" you are glad to see alive and who has a special place in your heart. I hugged Ralph every day that he came in, and I wasn't afraid to touch him because he certainly touched me in ways no words can express.

TALKING TO PEOPLE WHO ARE GRIEVING

Talking to people who are grieving is one of the most difficult things to do. I am a dog lover and if an animal dies it breaks my heart. My girlfriend Mona lost her dog, Gio. He was a two-year-old dog with a heart defect and he died of a heart attack. I was so devastated by this that I broke down immediately and cried in front of Mona, who was also grieving but in her own way. Her way was to hold it in and to grieve in private. My way was to grieve forcefully and openly.

There are no right or wrong ways to grieve. It comes from within. Everybody has their own individual way, and you need to respect that in the person and share in it with them. Don't be afraid to hug them if they want to be held. Comfort them. Be there for them. Take cues from the person, as some people want to be left alone. Most people want to be held and nurtured.

When a loss occurs, people feel empty so in order to fill the loss, physical contact is often important. It's important to allow the person to grieve and not to say things to still their emotions. You may even try to talk in joyous terms—acknowledging the loss but reminding the bereaved of the beautiful life the deceased had.

One of my clients was grieving hard for her sister who was ill for several years. She kept focusing on her sister's pain and her own guilt—that she didn't spend enough time with her sister. I then asked her to also remember how her sister Emily had a beautiful life filled with a mother, father, husband, brothers, and sisters who adored her. I reminded her of Emily's long, rich life and that now she didn't have to go through the excruciating pain she was in during her illness. Her sister was able to smile through her tears when she now focused on how happy her sister had been throughout her life.

So don't be afraid to say something beautiful, honest, and sincere about the person and their life and how they lived it. Of course, if a person was unkind, and you really didn't like them, you're better off not saying anything at all.

You also need to allow the person to get out all of their emotions. If they want to scream and yell, don't say, "Don't cry, it'll be o.k." Let them cry, scream, yell. It's devastating to have someone try to put your emotions in check because they may have difficulty dealing with their own emotions or grief.

When greeting the bereaved at a wake or a funeral, don't hold back in expressing your grief. Most people who have lost a loved one want to be held, hugged, kissed, and comforted. Most people want to be told how special and wonderful their loved one was. Let them know how that person touched your life and how much they meant to you. If you feel like crying— go ahead. Any way you express your grief is acceptable.

Nobody knows how they are going to react when they are first given the news that someone has died. Some people go into shock and are speechless and numb, while others wail and scream or even become ill. After you cope with your own grief, you need to make yourself readily available to the needs of the immediate family or loved ones. Tell them that you are available for them any time if they want to talk or if they want company. Ask if there is anything they would like for you to do. Ask if they need any food or help with any arrangements. If they reject your help, don't be offended. Just be there and be ready to offer your help again shortly after. All too often help is offered on the day of the funeral and afterwards the bereaved are neglected and not called. Therefore, it's a good idea to keep in touch with the bereaved. It not only helps you to work out your own grief but allows the bereaved to have a stronger support system during their time of emotional need.

TALKING TO PEOPLE WHO ARE MENTALLY ILL

One of the most difficult things to do is to communicate with people who are mentally ill. Oftentimes, you may think that a person is just hard to get along with and you end up treating them as if they are normal when in reality they are very ill.

The mother of a client of mine has a definite mental disorder. She is impulsive, abusive, hostile, hateful, and difficult to communicate with. One moment she's nice and the next moment she's mean. They have a roller-coaster relationship that is dysfunctional. My client has tried for years to get along with her mother, but it's been a losing battle and will always be because her mother is mentally ill.

You need to talk to people who are mentally ill very carefully. (1) Try not to raise your voice but be firm in your tone; (2) Get to the point immediately with them; (3) Set limits: Do not let them overstep your bounds; and (4) Limit your communication with them to the very basics.

I have heard so many sad stories of individuals having a spouse or a parent who is clearly mentally deranged, and the only way to deal with the person is to follow the above suggestions. Even though you may feel sorry for these people, their illness can ruin your life. Their pain may become your scars. For your own mental health, you may need to let go and only communicate with them through a qualified mental health professional. If circumstances don't permit them to get professional treatment, you need to limit your contact to essential encounters only or even get them completely out of your life, even though it may be one of the most difficult things for you to do.

TALKING TO PROFESSIONALS: DOCTORS, LAWYERS, C.P.A.s

So many people are intimidated by their doctors, dentists, lawyers, or C.P.A.s because they have advanced degrees, are bright, intelligent, and know a lot. Even though they are highly educated, they are still human beings, and mutual respect and consideration has to be maintained.

There are so many people who let doctors do procedures on them that they shouldn't let them do. People are overcharged by their lawyers or by their C.P.A.s just because they're afraid to speak up or they don't think that they have the right to—that if they offend their doctor or lawyer they won't find a new one. If you consider that these professionals are actually your employees—that they are working for you—you won't be intimidated by them.

A client of mine was going to a doctor to help her lose weight. This doctor was rude, obnoxious, and intimidating. He would say, "I can't believe you didn't lost a pound. How dare you? What did you eat?" Although he treated her with disrespect, she kept going back to him even though he intimidated her. She hated him and bad-mouthed him around town but stuck it out because she felt she had no choice. She did have a choice. Instead of bad-mouthing him she needed to say, "Look, Doctor, under no circumstances are you to speak to me that way. I respect you as a doctor, based on your training and ability, but you must respect me, too. Yes, I had a setback on your diet, but yelling at me and chastising me is unacceptable."

On the other hand, professionals may become antagonistic toward their client as a result of badgering questions they hear in defensive, argumentative tones. Monitoring your voice is important when you ask questions. Use key phrases like "Please explain what you mean." Take notes or ask if you can tape-record your conversation if you don't understand. Have them reiterate what you *specifically* don't comprehend. Use a calm, positive tone. Be completely *honest* and *open* about what you want from them and what you feel about them.

One of my clients was upset with a doctor I sent her to because she said he was abrupt and didn't spend enough time with her. I said, "Did he cure your problem?" "Yes," she replied, "but he only spent three minutes with me and charged me all this money." I said, "The reason this doctor charged you that much money is because he's that good and can diagnose a problem quickly and treat it, so what's the problem?" She smiled and said, "You're right. I guess he is good and that's why he is so busy." The main thing is not to keep these horrible feelings in but to confront what's bothering you. Oftentimes listening to an explanation can change your attitude.

TALKING TO SERVICE PEOPLE

All too often people who are employed in service positions—salespeople, waiters, waitresses—forget they are in a position to be helpful and of service to others. For whatever reason, some service people may take their frustrations our on their customers. Unfortunately, there is also a lot of routine snootiness or rudeness in very expensive stores. Perhaps this is to discourage buyers who are not serious from taking up salespeoples' time. But there is no excuse for such behavior. If you encounter rudeness, immediately let the salesperson know they are being offensive to you and that their behavior is unacceptable. Remind them that they are employed to help you—not to hinder you. Say, "I find your rudeness unacceptable." Often your making them aware of their rude behavior can change their attitudes as they realize they were out of line. If they get belligerent or continue to be rude, don't hesitate to get the manager and let them know what has occurred. Often this will take care of the problem. If not, go to the top—call the owner. Owners are in business to make money and want to know how you are treated. They know that poor treatment of customers results in poor sales. Don't just walk away and ignore rudeness. It is worth confronting anything that undermines your self-esteem. If more people spoke up and expressed how they felt, we would have fewer negative experiences in stores and restaurants. Oftentimes, just pointing out their impoliteness can immediately change their attitude so they become more of a help than a hindrance. Too many people don't say anything and harbor ill feelings and then never shop at a place again or eat at that restaurant again.

TALKING TO SUBORDINATES

People who get a position of authority, especially new bosses, sometimes feel that they have to be bossy. Being a boss means being respectful. When a person does something wrong, you don't rant and rave and scream and yell. A good boss is gracious and respectful but firm. Maids and secretaries are not slaves, and they need to be treated with respect and decency. One of my clients, a very wealthy, prominent man, had a son who was a "spoiled brat." His son was ordering the maids around when his father finally said to him, "Under no circumstances do you order our maids around. These are members of our household and you must treat them with respect. They are not your servants or slaves. Speak to them politely and never order them around."

This father was absolutely right. Treat everybody you come in contact with with respect. That is the secret of the most successful people in the world; people love working for them because they treat everyone with decency.

Why are Leona Helmsley and Zsa Zsa Gabor treated with such disdain in the press? It's because the press has reported that they are mean to the "little people"—the subordinates. In the book *Queen of Mean*, Leona Helmsley was said to treat her staff quite poorly. Countless newspaper articles likewise revealed that Zsa Zsa Gabor was similarly rude to people she employed. What they don't realize is that it is the "little people"—the cogs in the wheel—who make things move, who make them look good.

TALKING TO POLICE OFFICERS

Zsa Zsa Gabor made headlines across the world when she cursed and slapped a Beverly Hills police officer for pulling her over and giving her a ticket. As a result Zsa Zsa had to go to jail, pay a large fine, and do numerous hours of community service. Zsa Zsa is an example of how *never* to communicate with police officers. Most police officers are trained to be aware of how they communicate with the public. In fact, most police academies train their future officers to speak to others politely, even in making arrests. In addition, many police departments have employed psychologists and communications specialists to help teach courses in which officers learn to be effective when communicating with the public. They learn to help calm people down and reassure people who have been victimized by crimes.

On the other hand, there are some rude and nasty officers who obviously didn't pay attention during their courses. They unfortunately use their position as a "power trip." If this does happen, get the name and badge number and write a letter to their superior. Don't ignore their obnoxious behavior, but take care of your battle with them into the courtroom. Even if you feel like yelling at the officer—cursing them or slapping them—whatever you do DON'T because they have the authority and you don't.

If they are obnoxious, get their badge number and their name, and write a letter to their captain. If you have a witness, it gives your complaint even more credibility. So have them write a letter as well, documenting the officer's awful behavior. These letters are read and often go into the officer's file, which can affect his or her career advancement. Therefore, you do have some recourse to express how you were treated.

If you're pulled over, do not get out of the car unless you are asked. Say as little as possible. Just sit there and listen to what the officer says and only speak if he or she asks you a question. When you do address the officer, call him or her *officer* to show your respect for their position. Do the *Tension Blow-Out Exercise:* Take your breath in, hold it, and blow out all the air until your abdominal muscles contract. Then don't breathe for three seconds. Take the breath in, hold it, and repeat two more times until you've oxygenated yourself. It helps you control your temper so you won't antagonize the police officer, which can get you in trouble.

VOCAL SELF-DEFENSE

Unfortunately, we live in a society where crime has become all too rampant. In order to help deter someone from making you their crime victim, you need to learn some rules of vocal self-defense.

Several studies show that a person who walks like a victim— head bowed, slow gait, and poor posture—is more likely to be assaulted than one who projects a more confident presence. The same holds true for the way a person sounds. In fact, it can be the determining factor in whether they live or die.

For example, Alice, a twenty-eight-year-old client of mine, walked into her dark apartment one night only to find a would-be attacker who told her to take off her clothes. Luckily, Alice became calm and conscious of her breathing, and in soft, slow, reassuring tones she said, "Don't worry. I won't hurt you." This confused her attacker, which allowed her to escape successfully. In using a reassuring, soft tone, she was able to calm her attacker, which literally saved her life.

On the other hand, using a loud projected voice also saved a client's life. Jessica was engrossed in studying for an exam one night in an isolated area in the library. Suddenly she felt someone's hand grasping her ankle under the desk. Taking a breath in and tightening up her abdominal muscles, she let out with a loud, rich, booming voice, saying, "WHAT CAN I DO FOR YOU?" Her would-be attacker scurried away to find a more victim-like prey.

Besides using your voice appropriately, the main thing you need to do in deterring potential attackers is to be alert and mindful of everyone around you wherever you are, whether it be in elevators, buildings, garages, etc.

Unfortunately, most people who are the victims of a crime end up in shock—not being able to speak, move, or scream as the wind is oftentimes literally knocked out of them.

If, heaven forbid, you are victimized, try to remember to

(1) breathe rhythmically (in, hold, and slowly let it out) to oxygenate yourself; (2) try to stay calm and in control so your jabbering won't frighten the attacker and make them more nervous; and (3) only scream to get attention if you feel the situation warrants it. Otherwise, use soft, gentle, calming tones so that your life won't be in jeopardy. As difficult as it seems, try to keep your wits about you.

Here are some tips to remember so that you can help avoid being victimized.

1. Have upright posture with your head up. Use confident body language by acting like you know what you're doing or where you're going. Take longer steps when walking.

2. Be physically expansive as you take up more space, and don't let strangers invade your space. At all times, be aware of how close someone is to you.

3. Use deep, forceful tones if a stranger approaches you, and project your voice so you feel it resonating through your entire body.

4. Draw out your voice tones and sound more confident and self-assured. Use phrases like, "Nooo, gooo awaay," or "Stop it riiight nowww."

5. Use phrases like "What can *we* do for you?" if an unexpected visitor comes to your door. Saying *we* gives the impression you're not alone. Also, don't be intimidated into opening the door for an unexpected delivery person. Project your voice loudly, and use a short, staccato command like "Leave it on the front door." This can oftentimes save your life.

6. If you ask someone for directions or the time, use direct, confident questions. Don't act lost or insecure. Say, "What's the best way to get to Bedford Drive from here?" instead of "I can't seem to find Bedford Drive." Say, "What time is it?" instead of "I don't have a watch on me. Can you tell me what time it is?"

7. Finally, if you look at a person eye to eye and not shift your eyes away, you give the impression of confidence and self-assurance, making the would-be attacker think twice before bothering you.

... 13 ...

Sweet Talk

One of the most crucial aspects of communication is learning how to talk with someone with whom you are having a close personal relationship. Developing good communication skills is not easy. Communication becomes even more intense when emotions are involved. Marriage counselors and psychologists consistently report that the most common problem they see in relationships is the lack of communication. It's not surprising. Who teaches you how to talk to your mate? You fall in love, you're in bliss. You get married and now that you have to live together, what do you say? How do you talk with this special person in your life and maintain a good relationship?

This chapter is designed to help you learn how to talk to the people you are emotionally intimate with. You will learn what to say after you are attracted to another person, how to develop good interpersonal communications skills, how to discuss practically anything with your partner, and how to maintain open channels for good communication so that your relationship has the best chance of working. Finally, you will learn what to say in order to end a personal relationship where there is no hope.

MALE/FEMALE DIFFERENCES IN COMMUNICATION

A lot has been written about the differences between male and female communication. In fact, some researchers believe that the reason there are so many problems between couples is because of these differences. Many feel that we treat boy babies differently than we treat girl babies—that we speak in softer tones and verbalize more to girls than we do to infant boys. Neurological and developmental studies have shown that girls develop the left side of their brain faster than a boy of the same age does; hence girls develop language and speech skills sooner than boys.

Research also shows that boys and girls are socialized differently, as girls are treated more affectionately and are given more verbal approval. We have different expectations for girls than boys, even as indicated by their nursery rhymes.

Remember the nursery rhyme:

> *There was a little girl who had a little curl*
> *Right in the middle of her forehead,*
> *And when she was good, she was very, very good,*
> *But when she was bad, she was horrid.*

What did this little girl do that was so horrid? Did she squeal or jump up and down or have a mind of her own? We would certainly accept her behavior if she was a little boy rather than a little girl.

We also tend to pass on value judgments on the sex of our children without even realizing it, as illustrated by another popular nursery rhyme:

> *What are little girls made of?*
> *Sugar and spice and everything nice.*
> *What are little boys made of?*
> *Snips and snails and puppy dogs' tails.*

These sex differences even manifest themselves in what little girls and boys talk about. Studies show that little girls like to talk about people more—their friends, who and who likes who.

Since they tend to play together in twos, they like to tell each other secrets. This helps bond their friendship. On the other hand, studies show little boys are more apt to talk about things and activities. Since they tend to socialize in groups, they mostly talk about what they are all doing and who's the best and, of course, the biggest. These communication differences between boys and girls are carried over into puberty and later into adulthood.

Research has shown that the general conversation context among women outside the office or business sphere usually involves "people" and personal relationships, in both work and personal lives, "diet," "clothing," and "physical appearance." On the other hand, men usually talk about activities—sports or what was done at work, mechanical things, cars, news events, or music.

Not only do men and women talk about different things, but the manner in which they say things is entirely different. In fact, one of the foremost linguists, Robin Lakoff, says that women's language is almost different enough from men's to be a separate dialect. With so many biological, cultural, and social differences, it's not surprising that men and women have such a difficult time talking to one another.

However, you can overcome all of these sex differences if you can learn to say what you feel and express yourself honestly and openly. It's time to stop focusing on differences and focus on our similarities instead.

THE MAGIC OF VOCAL ATTRACTION

The excitement of being attracted to another person can literally take your breath away. In fact, research has shown that attraction as well as "falling in love" is a biochemical phenomenon. After you are initially attracted and you start talking to the person, you will know whether you'll continue to be attracted to them in a matter of a few minutes. After the first four minutes of a conversation, you'll know if a person is going to be your friend, your lover, or if you will ever have anything to do with them again.

Studies also show that even though you are first attracted to someone, you can quickly become unattracted to that person based on how they communicate with you—especially by the tone of their voice.

Oftentimes, it's not what a person says, but how they say it. In fact, this happened to a client of mine, Joyce, who saw her Adonis at the hors d'oeuvres table. She was initially attracted to him, but when she went over to talk to him and heard a high-pitched weak voice, she was no longer interested. Similarly, a client of mine, Patricia, was fixed up with her "ideal man," according to her best friend. He certainly was her ideal man on paper. He had all the attributes she wanted—good job, athletic ability, great dresser, nice car, but when she met him in person it was another story. After the first minute she regretted even opening the door and letting him in. He was such a monotonous bore with no life in the way he talked. He sounded empty and hollow. She couldn't wait for the date to be over.

Her date was an interesting man, but because he sounded like a lifeless bore, she didn't even give him a chance. One can't blame her. Patricia was reacting to her date's annoying speech habits, which can have a deleterious effect on not only the person who has these habits, but on the person who has to listen to these annoying speech habits.

Most of the time, when we are turned off by the way a person talks, we don't understand exactly what it is that annoys us. The Gallup Organization surveyed men and women from all over the United States, ranging in age from eighteen-years-olds to senior citizens, and representing all levels of income and education. People in the survey were asked about eleven frequently encountered talking habits. Did they find the habits annoying, and how much? This unique poll gives us a powerful tool for understanding exactly what it is about our speech that can cause the most problems for us. Here are the results of the survey. The numbers are the percentages of those polled.

GALLUP POLL RESULTS

	Totally Annoyed	Does Not Annoy	Don't Know
Interrupting while others are talking	88	11	1
Swearing or curse words	84	15	1
Mumbling or talking too softly	80	20	0
Talking too loudly	73	26	1
Monotonous, boring voice	73	26	1
Using filler words such as "and um," "like um," and "you know"	69	29	2
A nasal whine	67	29	4
Talking too fast	66	34	0
Using poor grammar or mis-pronouncing words	63	36	1
A high-pitched voice	61	37	2
A foreign accent or a regional dialect	24	75	1

As you can see, close to seventy-three percent of the people surveyed were turned off by boring monotones, so now you can see why Patricia couldn't give her date a chance. His tone annoyed her so much that she didn't even want to know him.

Elaine is loud and boisterous and wonders why she was never picked at the video-dating service she belongs to—even though she's got a great face, great clothes, and a great body.

Even though someone maybe physically attracted to you, if you die off at the end of sentences, talk too loud, sound nasal and whining, and have a too high-pitched voice, interrupt a lot, or talk too fast, you aren't going to remain attractive to them.

What makes a person stay attractive is a warm, sensuous, vivacious voice with good eye contact and meaningful communication. If you think back to your high school and college days to who was the most popular girl or boy at school, you will recall that it was the one who had the best communications skills. It wasn't necessarily the one who had the best body or face. It was the one who had the best way of making other people feel comfortable. The warm people were often the popular people.

In order to make people feel comfortable around you, you need to follow these steps.

- Be expressive
- Have good eye contact
- Use modulated tones
- Be interested and not interesting
- Let the other person finish—don't interrupt
- Ask questions, but not too many—don't be invasive
- Have a warmth to your tone of voice—a sincerity where you care not only about what you are talking about but about what the other person is saying.

When you are mutually attracted, you'll both know it because people who are mutually attracted smile more, they react more to each other, and they have more consistent eye contact. Tell the other person "I'm really attracted to you. I find you so attractive." If you feel uncomfortable being that direct, say, "I really relate to you," or "I feel a kinship with you." Most people aren't used to being that direct. In fact, many might feel that if they are that direct the other person might feel they are giving them a line.

Perhaps the reason people feel so uncomfortable being honest and direct is because they've read so many books that plot "how to get your man" or find the "woman of your dreams," which in essence tell them how to cheat and manipulate to find Mr. or Mrs. Right. For example, they tell you how to dress to please your man and mirror his behavior so that he will like you. If you're not *completely* honest and up front initially and you do succeed in finding your mate after following these cookbook

196 · LILLIAN GLASS, PH.D.

approaches you read about, you won't be able to maintain the relationship.

Based on thousands of hours of talking to people as a communications specialist, I have learned that the only way any relationship is going to work is if two people are mutually open and have honest, up-front communication. In essence, you let the other person know who you are, and you in turn have to know who they are.

FLIRTING

A great deal has been written about flirting. In fact there are books teaching people how to flirt. How-to-flirt workshops have even made the seminar circuit across the country. Your initial reaction to all of this might be negative as you associate the flirting with guile, deceit, and manipulation. You may even recall the "flirt" in high school who teased and manipulated to get attention.

Even though the connotation we have of flirting is negative, flirting can be a positive and a fun experience, provided there are limits. There is one essential rule when you flirt: Never start anything you can't finish. This means don't lead anyone on. Compliment them, nurture them, but don't encourage or mislead them if there is no hope.

For example, flirting allows you to take some risks and to take charge of your life and to meet new people. Flirting can also help you use better eye contact, and to return another person's glances. All too often when someone is attracted to us we will avert our eyes and look down. No eye contact is made because of our shyness or our feeling uncomfortable by returning the glance. Oftentimes, too many of us lose out on connecting with the person who was attracted to us because they assume *we* are not interested in *them*.

Flirting can also encourage you to smile—which signals openness and receptivity. It encourages warmth, friendliness, a sense of humor, and attentiveness.

The most important thing to remember if you're going to flirt is to be sincere. Be real. Give *honest* compliments and stay away from "lines." Most of us can certainly detect insincerity.

One of my clients told me about a charming man she met at a party who kept saying wonderful things to her—making her feel like the most important person. When she returned from the ladies' room, she overheard him giving another woman the same lines he had just given her. She was so turned off by his insincerity that she refused to give him her phone number at the end of the party.

Another big turnoff is saying something critical or sarcastic and trying to be funny in order to attract the other person's attention. This usually backfires. They may not realize that you're trying to be humorous because they may not share your sense of humor. When you are being sarcastic you aren't being direct, honest, and sincere so you can't expect someone to be that receptive to you.

COMING ON AND BACKING OFF

More often than not the situation is that you'll meet someone that you're attracted to and it's not reciprocated. Let's say you were on an airplane sitting next to a handsome gentleman and he was reading a newspaper. You want to strike up a conversation with him but he won't respond. Before you start feeling rejected, take a breath in, hold it, and congratulate yourself for getting out there and trying—for taking a risk. Maybe he's involved with someone else or is pre-occupied with something that has *nothing* to do with you. So don't take the rejection so personally.

If you keep sending out cues that you're interested in a person and it's not reciprocated, stop! Don't try to convince the person they need to know you, or make a pest of yourself. Get the hint and back off. Even though it may sound corny, "There certainly are other fish in the sea."

Sometimes the person may be attracted to you but they may need time. They may be so shy that you may get the impression that they aren't interested. It's up to them to make the next move. The signals they are putting out are that they are not interested, so respect them. If they are interested and eventually get the nerve to respond to you, they will let you know.

On the other hand, it's important to be polite and smile at someone who is complimenting you or who is attracted to you. It doesn't hurt to say, "Thank you" when anyone says something kind to you. If you're not attracted to them, you may just want to limit your response to the "Thank you" and not give them any additional encouragement—eye contact or conversation. If the person doesn't pick up on your cues and nonreaction, then you need to spell it out to them more clearly. Using polite tones, phrases such as "Thank you very much, but I am not available," or "You're kind but I really can't talk to you anymore" will usually give them the message. If they still persist, raise the volume of your voice, maintain eye contact, and in a firm voice say: "I told you I am not interested! Please leave me alone!" If that doesn't work, let the person know how obnoxious they are being and leave.

WHAT TO SAY WHEN YOU CLICK

In today's society, it's oftentimes difficult to tell if someone is interested in you. There are so many nuances or subtle clues. Someone may just be flirting with you to build up their own ego or to pass time.

One of my octogenarian clients told me that when she was a single young girl she and her single girlfriends would take a stroll after dinner. It was customary to drop a handkerchief in front of a man that you were attracted to. As he picked it up, the woman would smile and bow her head coquettishly, indicating a cue to the gentleman that he could call upon her to ask her out for a date—a simple, elegant form of communication. It was easy to tell if there was mutual interest.

Today we have different sets of rules. If we see someone we like, we glance at them a few seconds longer than usual, then we avert our eyes. Then we look again, to see if they are looking at us. If they are interested and our eyes meet, we maintain our eye contact and then smile. This is a cue that we want to talk. When you click with someone, you just know it! A comfortable feeling comes over you. You don't have to impress, cajole, or work so hard to get the person to notice you. You can express yourself freely even if you don't agree with the other person.

The conversation flows, and gestures and body language are natural.

Being mutually attracted to another person is one of life's special moments. When you click with another person, you'll find that you can't seem to get that smile off of your face because you've found something mutually familiar and exciting.

When it comes to men or women asking one another out—there are *no rules*. If you're attracted to someone, it doesn't matter what sex you are; you just need to be open and honest and non-threatening. Allow the other person to say "no" and yourself to "save face" if they aren't interested. Don't keep persisting. If you've asked someone out three times and they have an excuse each time without giving you an alternative, stop asking.

For example, if you ask someone to dinner and they say, "No, I can't—I'm busy that day," and then you repeat this scenario three times, chances are they don't want to go out with you at all. If on the other hand they say, "Oh, I'd love to go out but I'm busy that day—how about next week?" you can rest assured that they are interested in seeing you.

Oftentimes, it's best to go to coffee or lunch with a person. It gives you a better chance to get to know them without pressure. It's a non-threatening situation.

If, on the other hand, someone asks you out and you don't want to go out with them—don't try to be nice and not hurt their feelings by saying, "Sure, another time," and not really mean it. Being direct, honest, and open hurts them less in the long run than stringing them along. Use phrases such as "No, thank you. I'm flattered but I am not available to go out with you," or "I don't think we ought to pursue this further," or "Why don't I contact you if I decide to go out with you?" This way everything is up front and out in the open and there are no hurt feelings.

GETTING TO KNOW THEM

Asking a person out was so much easier when you were in high school or college where you knew the person's character, their friends, and their background. When we're out of school we don't have that luxury so it's important to find out as much as you can about the person. You need to be open and direct and not worry if you are being too nosey or inquisitive. In this day and age you need to know before whom you stand!

If you ask someone an intimate question, be prepared to accept the answer. For example, if you ask someone if they've ever tried drugs and they answer that they had a serious heroin problem, don't ignore and gloss over what they just said because you fear they might feel uncomfortable talking about it. If they brought it up, pursue it—continue to ask questions like, "When did you get over your problem?" or "How did you get started?" until *they* don't want to answer your questions any longer. Let *them* make the decision. On the other hand, don't make judgmental comments like "How sick!" or "I hate drug addicts!" If they felt comfortable sharing this personal information with you, then you need to respect that and not make them feel uncomfortable for sharing the intimacy with you.

Oftentimes direct, open questioning gives you data you need to decide whether or not you want that person in your life. However, in order to learn about a person, you don't necessarily always have to ask about personal and intimate things. Discussing world affairs, sports, business, news, and entertainment can give you insight. Being a good listener and paying careful attention to what they say can give you further insight into who they are and how they see the world and themselves. For example, if they constantly put themselves down and say terrible things about themselves, they are revealing low self-esteem.

Usually people will reveal everything you want to know. Listen for consistencies in what they tell you. Listen to their belief systems as they tell you about certain situations they have been involved in. Listen to how they approach problems in their life. Even though it takes time to really get to know a person, your sharp listening skills combined with direct and open questioning can allow you to quickly discover how much you both share in common. It will also enable you to determine whether it's worth investing the time and energy to pursue the relationship.

ENDING A RELATIONSHIP— TELLING SOMEONE IT'S OVER

We have all heard the expression "It takes two to tango." Just as you need another person who knows how to do the tango to dance with, you need another person who is open and receptive to talk with and have a successful relationship with. If you don't have good communication, you have an empty relationship. Oftentimes, you are better off without a relationship if that relationship destroys your self-esteem.

For years Marlene tried everything possible to save her ten-year-marriage to Bill. Bill was always critical of her, even in public. He hardly ever talked to her except to tell her about dinner or plans or what he decided they would do. He always seemed to be in a bad mood and seemed to blame her for everything that went wrong. Marlene took all of this "for the sake of the children" and "for the sake of their finances."

She wanted to make this marriage work. She attended workshop after workshop, read book after book, and saw therapist after therapist—alone. When she asked Bill to go with her for marriage counseling his reply was, "You're the one who needs help—not me. I'm not going to any counselor."

For whatever reasons, the clear lack of communication between them made Marlene feel like she was "dancing the tango alone." She felt as though there was no hope. Finally, she had no recourse. She made up her mind to tell Bill that the relationship was over—but didn't know how to do it. My advice to her was to be honest and direct and to speak from her heart— her *own* experiences. She took my suggestion and confronted Bill that night.

She told Bill, "I am terribly unhappy. I can't live in this relationship anymore because my self-esteem is suffering. I've tried to do everything I knew how, but *our* inability to communicate *together* leaves me no choice but to end this marriage and I've made arrangements with my lawyer."

As soon as she told Bill it was over she felt an immediate surge of relief and excitement about starting her new life.

Most situations may not be as extreme as Marlene and Bill's. However, when you have been ambivalent about a relationship and then finally made up your mind to end it after all else has failed, you need to use the *direct, honest approach.*

1. Confront your mate as calmly as possible. Use the relaxation breathing technique to help calm you down.
2. Maintain direct eye contact at all times.
3. Be direct and to the point.
4. Express how *you* feel—how the marriage has affected *you* and how *you* want out.
5. Confront without accusations and vehemence.

You have to *confront* the situation *directly* and *honestly.* Keep in mind "the relationship is over." It is terribly sad—like a death. Mourn it in any way you know how. Take as long as you need. When you're ready—move on! Never look back because it is the best decision you've ever made. For many, it's better to live with less than to live with someone whom you can't communicate with—someone who chips away at your self-esteem and destroys who you are.

Most often when you've directly confronted and ended a toxic relationship, you'll find that your life becomes even more successful. You may become more motivated, more creative, and even more excited about life. This in turn will allow you to make even more money, have more friends, and have an even richer life than you had before.

Oftentimes, verbally confronting a toxic relationship and leaving it behind brings you a newfound sense of inner strength to carry with you throughout your life. After all, if you could confront one of the most difficult situations in your life and handle it—you can confront and do anything!

TEN KEYS TO MAINTAINING A GOOD RELATIONSHIP THROUGH GOOD COMMUNICATION SKILLS

After spending literally thousands of hours listening to people talk about their personal relationships, I've come up with ten essential rules to live by if you plan to have a nurturing relationship where your love can grow.

1. KEEP TALKING

The number-one complaint I hear between couples is "We don't talk anymore." All too often couples take one another for granted. When they do, the communication stops. In order to have a good relationship, you have to keep talking to one another *regularly*. No matter how busy you are or how little time you have, you need to make time to talk. Even if it's fifteen minutes a day, you need to let your partner know how you are and what you've been up to and find out how they are and what they've been up to. You need to share things on a daily basis that concern you both. Absence of communication definitely does not "make the heart grow fonder." Instead, it distances the both of you so after a while it is as though you begin to lead separate lives.

When you talk to your mate, don't just present a series of facts regarding what you did that day. Instead, express how you felt about what you did and describe your emotions. Use more visual, auditory, or olfactory descriptions. This helps your partner share the experience with you more completely and feel like he or she was actually there with you. It makes them feel more a part of your world.

Even something as mundane as going to the grocery store can interest your partner if you describe your experience using all of your senses. Saying "I went to the grocery store" is not as effective as saying "I went to the grocery store and I was exhausted until I walked in the middle of all the pastries and the great smell woke me up. I got so hungry that I ate one of the cream-filled Danishes I bought for us right there in the store."

Another thing to keep in mind is that your mate is not a *mind reader*. There is nothing more annoying than to ask your partner what's wrong (when you know something is—based on their body and face language and attitude) only to hear "nothing." You ask again and hear the same reply. When this happens, you need to confront your mate directly, honestly, openly, and lovingly. Mirror what behavior of theirs you are seeing by saying, "Honey, I know something is wrong because you don't look happy. Is there something you'd like to share with me?" or "I'm on your side so if there's something you'd like to talk about, I want you to know that I'm here for you."

Unfortunately, a lot of people aren't used to opening up and sharing—especially on emotionally laden issues. Many were raised in homes where they were conditioned to hold things in—not to express their feelings and keep a stiff upper lip. Therefore, it's up to you to *help* your mate learn to be open. Let them know that it's safe to do so. Oftentimes, clients who have employed these techniques with their mates have reported remarkable results as they have felt a greater sense of closeness with their partner.

If your partner still won't talk, help them out by saying what you think is bothering them and then ask them if you're on the right track.

2. LISTEN

Even though we will talk more about how to be a good listener in chapter 15, being a good listener is essential if you want to have a good relationship.

An all too common complaint among couples is "He or she never pays attention to what I have to say." In order for any personal relationship to work out, both partners have to pay close attention to what the other says and remember what was said. If you want a loving relationship, always be receptive to hearing the details of your partner's experiences. Don't tune out or turn off when your loved one needs to talk. If it is an inopportune time to talk, say something like, "Honey, now isn't a good time for me to listen to you. I really want to hear everything you have to say to me so I'd like you to tell me this *afternoon*, so you can have all of my attention." That afternoon make sure you then get back to your mate and take the time to listen.

Really listening not only to what your partner has to say, but how they say it, serves as an emotional barometer that can alert you to any problems they may be having. You can become a more responsive partner when you really listen openly and sympathetically. You learn more from one another when you listen.

Finally, don't interrupt. Keep listening until your partner has finished talking.

3. BE DIRECT—CONFRONT

You need to confront—stop "beating around the bush" and get to the point. Never put your requests in question form instead of making a direct statement. For example: "Wouldn't it be nice if we could go out to dinner and maybe a movie?" is less effective than saying "Honey, I'd like to go to a movie and dinner." Make yourself clear and be very specific when you express what your needs are.

If you're curious about how your partner thinks or feels, don't assume anything. Ask directly and honestly and openly. Direct communication not only saves time but helps to eliminate any anxieties you may have regarding how your partner feels about something. Even though you may hear something you don't particularly like, at least now you know where they stand so you no longer have to worry about it.

4. SHARING INTIMATE SECRETS

Intimate communication is sharing your worst and best thoughts and secrets with your partner. In turn, it is having your partner accept those thoughts and secrets. The more often you share, the closer you become.

The happiest couples I have seen in my practice are the ones who share everything and have no secrets. They are *completely* honest and open. They can talk about anything from the state of their bowels to their past affairs. They keep no secrets and tell no lies.

Even though many books on the market tell you *not* to share your innermost thoughts—to remain a mystery—I completely disagree! Withholding information can create distance between couples while sharing intimacies can only bring you closer.

The only time sharing an intimacy can be a problem is when your partner throws your secret back at you as ammunition during an argument or even teases you about it. This is completely unacceptable and can lead to major scars in a relationship.

In an intimate moment, Diane shared her lifelong secret of bulimia with Eric. Eric, feeling equally close, shared his secret of wetting his bed until he was thirteen. A few weeks later Diane bought some new satin sheets for their bed and, thinking she was being cute, said to Eric as she was putting the new sheets on the bed, "Now these sheets are expensive, so don't ever wet on these." As she laughed, Eric felt sick to his stomach. He couldn't believe how insensitive Diane could be by saying what she did. It put a wedge between them that was difficult to repair. Eric now felt he could never share anything with Diane again for fear she would throw it back at him. He felt that he could no longer trust her.

So, under any circumstances, never throw an intimate secret back at your partner if you want to maintain trust.

5. APOLOGIZING—LOVE IS HAVING TO SAY YOU'RE SORRY

In the early 1970s we all heard the phrase "Love is never having to say you're sorry," based on the popular movie, *Love Story*. Well, love is definitely having to say you're sorry in the 1990s. When you love someone there is no ego involved, only honest, open communication. Love is letting your partner know when you have made that mistake and how bad you feel about what happened between the two of you.

I can't begin to recount the number of times I have heard a disgruntled husband or wife say to me, "If only they would say they were sorry for what they did. Then it would show me how terrible they feel about what happened." If you've done something wrong—something you feel sad about—readily admit it, say you're sorry, and mean it!

6. DON'T DEMAND/DON'T COMMAND

We've all heard the expression "You can get more flies with honey than with vinegar." Sweet speech, flavored with terms of politeness, love, and endearment, produces far more positive results than acidy speech peppered with demands.

You need to be aware not only of *what* you say but *how* you say it. Sometimes we put out direct commands and demands and we're not even aware of it.

For example, a husband might come home from work and say to his wife, "Get me a beer." Her immediate reaction to his command is totally negative and hostile as she replies, "Get it yourself. I'm not your slave—what happened to your legs? You can walk, so get it yourself." Not knowing why she has flown off the handle, he is perplexed and says, "What's wrong with you? Is a lousy can of beer too much to ask for?" "No," she replies sharply, "but I'm not your maid."

The wife is reacting not to what her husband said but to *how* he said it. The command "Get me a beer" triggered her hostility. Had he couched his request in terms of endearment, "Sweetheart, would you mind please getting me a beer?" he probably would have his beer in his hand.

For positive results in communicating with your mate, *never* command or demand; instead, use lots of "honeys," "sweethearts," "loves," "pleases," and "thank yous."

7. DON'T NAG, ACCUSE, BLAME OR CRITICIZE

If you want a loving and supportive relationship, don't accuse or criticize or nag. Doing these things on a consistent basis are sure ways to end a relationship and even a destroy a sex life.

Granted, it's hard to accept some things your mate does, and you definitely need to tell them what irks you. However, don't do it in a way that completely destroys their self-esteem. Even though you might be annoyed and frustrated about what they've done, don't berate them or fight like siblings. Before you are ready to nag, accuse, criticize, or blame, just think back to what you liked about your mate that brought you together in the first place—the positive things you fell in love with.

When you do tell them what you're not happy with, don't whine, or pout, or use sharp tones.

Instead of saying, "You never take me anywhere; you're always out with your friends," attribute your feelings to yourself and use "I" instead of "you." Instead, say, "I feel sad that we never go out anymore. I'd love it if we'd spend more time together." "I get depressed when I see you smoking and drinking."

Describe how their actions affect you instead of directly attacking them and putting them on the defensive.

8. BE GENEROUS IN YOUR COMPLIMENTS

Free-flowing, sincere compliments colored with descriptive adjectives will greatly enhance communication between you and your partner. Complimenting your partner often and really noticing even their slightest accomplishments and improvements with a verbal pat on the back will usually make them feel you are being more attentive and supportive.

Don't be stingy with your compliments—elaborate when you like something. For example, if your wife has spent time getting dressed and asks, "How do I look?" don't just say "fine" or "nice." Her response might well be, "If you don't like the way I look, why don't you say so." Confused by this you may then say, "I said you looked nice—what do you expect me to say?"

You're expected to more fully express yourself and elaborate. For example, you may say, "You look so beautiful tonight. I love how your blue dress brings out the color in your eyes."

9. PUT SPARKLE IN YOUR TONE

It's often not what you say, but how you say it that can bring about a negative reaction. Saying "I love you" in a dull, lifeless, boring monotone will clearly not bring about the same response as an "I love you" said with enthusiasm, life, and meaning. In order to have better communication with your partner, you need to be in touch with all of your emotions—fear, love, happiness, sadness, doubt, boredom, compassion, and sympathy.

Your voice needs to reflect the life of these emotions when you speak so that you can express yourself more deeply and more effectively.

Finally, use an upward inflection or an upward bounce to show excitement when you first see your loved one. Don't use a boring monotone that gives the impression that you've taken them for granted.

10. BE GENEROUS IN YOUR BODY LANGUAGE

Not only do you need to keep talking in order to maintain a good relationship—you need to keep touching. You need to regularly hug and put your arms around your partner—even if it's for no reason at all. Touch your partner's arm or cheek or shoulder to further stress a point. Maintain direct eye contact and focus on your partner's eyes as you speak. Doing this on a regular basis creates a stronger bond between you and your mate.

... 14 ...

Your Opinion/My Opinion

If two or more intelligent people get together, more often than not there will be a difference of opinion. Because of the varied experiences and situations we have encountered throughout our lives, it is inevitable that two people will not always see something from the same viewpoint. Although I strongly believe one must express their opinion and say how they feel and not necessarily agree with the other person just to make them feel good, I do feel that you have to disagree with another person without offending or alienating them.

Saying "You stupid jerk," or "You idiot," or "You're crazy," or "You don't know what you're talking about" is definitely unacceptable.

I once had a client who was the most opinionated, cranky old man I had ever met. He was a know it all who thought he was always right. He was so full of venom that when he spoke it even affected his vocal cords. His lifetime habit of screaming at other people and using harsh tones played havoc on his raw, nodulated vocal cords. His constant arguing with people manifested itself in his emotional, mental, and physical health.

After teaching him how to produce more positive, loving tones and not to be so quick to always be right and fight with everyone, his life began to change. The turning point was when I videotaped him and he actually saw himself arguing with himself. He was shocked as he saw how his belligerent, hostile tones alienated other people, and how he approached every topic with hostility and anger in his voice. Seeing himself literally changed his negative behavior overnight.

You can disagree with somebody, but you don't have to verbally rip their heads off. You don't have to humiliate them.

Ralph Waldo Emerson had a great saying about people who had two different points of view. He said, "If I do not believe as you believe, and you do not believe as I believe, all it shows is that I don't believe as you believe and you don't believe as I believe." This quote is important to remember whenever you are talking to another person who may have a different opinion than you. If you are vehement and hostile about your belief system, the other person will not even hear what you have to say. You always need to respect the other person and use key phrases, such as:

- "I understand what you are saying . . ."
- "Try to look it at from my point of view for a moment . . ."
- "I respect what you are saying, but here is another way of looking at it . . ."
- "I want us to work this out. Let's see if we can find some common ground."

Avoid adamant statements like, "You don't know what you are talking about" or "I know I'm right," which further alienate people and make the communications gap wider.

One of my clients, Carol, is a highly opinionated woman from the East Coast. She always thinks her way is the right way. Because she has been married for ten years, she thinks she has all the right answers regarding relationships. If a friend tells her about a problem in their relationship, she immediately presents her opinion in a harsh, dominating, condescending way. She attacks the person and makes them feel stupid for what they have said or done. This "know it all" has alienated so many people that nobody likes to talk to her. The fact that she puts her two cents in is not a problem. The problem is *how* she does it.

Certainly, when two people get together and have differences of opinion tempers can fly, and people tend to get overly emotional. In order to avoid emotional flareups, two people have to consciously speak in terms that don't incite one other. That means they have to keep calm, as difficult as it may seem, and they need to be respectful of one another at all times.

Respect for another person is the only thing you need to keep in mind, no matter how angry or how awful you feel about a situation. One of my clients, a writer, was involved in a project with another writer. The two of them were literally at each other's throats because of a difference of opinion about how to approach a project. The arguments were getting way out of line—there was screaming and a lot of animosity going on between the two—when my client finally said to his co-writer, "Look, I have too much respect for you to let this happen between us. I don't want us to be ugly with one another."

It was the word "respect" that broke down the wall of negativity between the two of them, and they were once again able to work with one another, this time with a better understanding of what each had to offer in the way of strengths to the project. In essence, they allowed each other to "save face."

A GOOD ARGUMENT

Believe it or not, arguing can be good for you. In fact, research shows that more marriages break up when two people *avoid* arguing with each other than when they are able to express their feelings openly, even if they are angry.

In order to have a good marriage, or any good relationship, for that matter, it is essential for you to get your feelings out, for you to express your emotions and say what is really going on inside of you. This doesn't mean becoming a warrior and attacking the other person with verbal violence.

Instead, you need to express what the other person is *doing* that you don't like, not what that person *is* that you don't like. You need to confront their *actions*, as opposed to *who they are* as a person.

Most people don't know how to argue. They rant and rave and bring up things from the past. They often don't stick to the issue at hand. They pull out verbal ammunition that has nothing to do with the problem at hand. This is unfair and is what usually destroys relationships because there tends to be a resulting lack of trust.

For example, let's say your husband forgot your birthday. Of course, you are feeling very hurt, and even angry. In order to argue fairly, you need to express the fact that birthdays mean a lot to you and how his missing your birthday has made you feel—empty, alone, alienated, abandoned, and terribly sad. An unfair argument would be to tell him how he never remembers anything. In fact, last week he forgot to pick up the dog from the vet. And everyone in his family is an insensitive, thoughtless jerk, and he obviously inherited his thoughtlessness and lack of sensitivity from them.

So while research has shown that arguing can be good for you, the wrong kind of arguing—dragging someone out on the carpet for every bad thing they ever did to you for a single offense—can only be destructive.

Another bit of advice for good arguing is that *less is more.* When you begin, try to say what is bothering you in as few words as possible, and then go on and elaborate. Besides giving you a chance to gather your thoughts, this gives the other person a "preview" of what is bothering you. If they know what is coming because you got to the point, they will be less likely to be apprehensive and more apt to listen to what your complaints are.

Sometimes you may get into a heated discussion: There's nothing wrong with that. If you have to yell, go ahead and yell. Get it out. Just don't attack the other person. Don't accuse them. This will only make the other person feel defensive. Instead, concentrate on expressing your emotions by telling the other person how their *actions* have made you feel.

The appropriate time to express your emotions is when you are feeling them, but it also has to be at a situationally appropriate moment. For example, if you are at church, it may not be the right time to express your anger. However, you don't want to let too much time pass before letting someone know that something they have done disturbs you.

If you are angry about something, you have to let the other person know immediately—not ten minutes later, not an hour later, and not a day later, and definitely not a week later. Handle things as soon as possible.

A client of mine, who is a successful, superb actor, was recently in a movie that I worked on with him. The movie didn't turn out that well due to a weak script, an impossible director, and a poor editor. However, I thought that my client did a wonderful job. He was the consummate professional who did the best he could to portray the character under the circumstances. A friend of mine, knowing that I work with this client, said, "Did you see how horrible your client was in that movie?" My maternal, protective instincts came out and I rushed to defend my client, blaming it on the editing, rather than his performance. My friend continued to state their opinion, stating that they thought he was overdramatic in his portrayal of the character. I said, "I remember the scene you are talking about, and I respect your opinion. I also respect you as well. But I want you to respect my feelings as someone who worked closely with the project, and I feel my client's performance was terrific considering the circumstances and the pressures he had to work under."

My friend was able to hear what I had to say and ended up seeing my point of view after all.

When I was in junior high school, I remember a very big fistfight two boys had about whether a Ford or a Chevy was the better car. The most amazing thing about this incident was that the entire class took sides, and soon everyone was involved in a free-for-all brawl. Just because there was a difference of opinion and no other way of expressing one's view, the argument degenerated into the ultimate breakdown of communication—a physical fight.

Unfortunately, this doesn't just happen to twelve-year-old boys. Look at the bitter divorce battles that plague our society. Look at the fighting that is going on all over the world, with people killing each other just because they don't share the same opinion and they can't talk about it.

As a communications specialist, I believe that all communication problems are solvable. I have found that there are seven points that you need to follow in order to solve arguments and promote good communication.

1. Don't raise your voice. Even though you are emotionally tuned in, a calm, deliberate tone will allow you to be heard.

2. Always respect the other person's opinion and values, and as difficult as it may seem, try to see it from their point of view.

3. Under no circumstances are you to interrupt. Bite your tongue if you have to control yourself, but let the person speak their mind. If emotionally laden words trigger certain buttons, jot down the points, *do not* interrupt.

4. Use key phrases, such as "I understand what you are saying . . . I can see your point of view . . . I respect what you are saying, however . . ." Let the person know that *you* actually have heard them.

5. Summarize in your own words what the other person said so that you can both make sure you heard each other's points accurately.

6. After you have summarized, find a common point of reference—a point where each of you agree and are literally speaking the same language.

7. Then present your point of view, and ask the person to summarize how they perceived what you have said.

This may seem like a simplistic seven-step formula, but it works. I have encouraged my clients to use it, and they have had enormous success. They find themselves better equipped to get along both in business and in their interpersonal relationships. Clients who hadn't spoken to their enemies or family members for years were able to finally break through communications barriers employing these seven steps.

HOW TO AVOID HURTING OTHERS WITH YOUR OPINIONS

In previous chapters we've talked about knowing before whom you stand. Before you give your honest opinion and open yourself up to potential debate, you may want to *know your audience.*

Even though you are entitled to your opinion, you have to express it when it's situationally appropriate, and when it is in everyone's best interest.

I have learned this on a personal level from spending many years working with clients. They may have performed poorly at our sessions, they may not have sounded very good, they may not have been able to grasp what to do to improve themselves. I've learned a great deal about how important patience can be and how important tact and diplomacy is. I have also employed the seven-step program to help my clients be the best they can be. When people come into my office to solicit my opinion about their total image—their speech, their dress, the way they present themselves—they will often feel vulnerable and naked. The last thing they need is someone who is not sensitive to their feelings.

If, in the course of my evaluation, I have to tell them something about themselves that may not be very flattering, I will often use the expression, "Let's put our egos in our back pocket and pretend we are looking at a third person. I'm not here to offend you or hurt your feelings, because I'm on your side."

Saying this to my clients works extremely well as it gives them more confidence and allows them to see themselves more objectively. It also helps to avoid any hurt feelings or any misunderstanding or feeling that someone is humiliating or embarrassing them.

In voicing your opinion you have to avoid humiliating the other person: Be able to have them really listen to what you have to say to them, and finally create a situation where they can take your advice. This can be accomplished by first and foremost respecting the other person as a human being, using warm vocal tones, having consistent eye and facial contact, using a firm resonant voice, and calmly explaining your point of view by stating the facts as you see them and explaining how the facts make you feel.

Even if someone solicits your opinion, and you are not a trained professional, you may want to think twice before you "put your two cents in." Before you give an opinion, you have to be prepared to acknowledge that your relationship may be on the line.

Giving unsolicited opinions is what usually causes arguments. Most people feel that they are doing their "friends" a big service by telling them how they honestly feel about a situation, but most of the time they are not. They are actually turning their friends off and creating a lot of hard feelings.

If you want to put your two cents in, the first thing you need to do is "couch" what you say with, "May I put my two cents in?" or "I don't want this to affect our friendship, but do you want me to tell you how I feel about this situation?" Oftentimes, it's not *what* you say, but *how* you say it that can create an argument and even ruin a relationship.

For example, if you don't like the man your friend is dating, you don't want to say, "I can't stand that disgusting man you go out with. He's nothing but a drunken bum." You only want to give your opinion if it is solicited, and then you want to couch it with a great deal of sensitivity. In fact, if you don't like who the person is involved with, you may want to feel them out by asking them, "How do *you* feel about your relationship? Do you feel that you are getting a lot out of being with this person? How does he or she make you feel when you are around them?"

You don't want to put your unwelcome two cents in, which could destroy your friendship forever—especially when it concerns emotional issues such as a couple's relationship.

No matter how bad a relationship appears to you, when two heads are on the same pillow, there is another level of communication that you are totally unaware of. So what you see is not always what the real relationship is all about anyway. So keep your opinions—especially negative ones—to yourself.

HOW TO AVOID GETTING DRAWN INTO AN ARGUMENT

One of my clients, Gloria, came in one day feeling proud of herself for handling a situation between herself and her sister, Barbara, and for not allowing herself to be drawn into an argument.

She told me how Barbara had come crying to her about her horrible husband, and how she couldn't live with him anymore. "He always puts me down," she had said. "He never lets me do what I want. I feel so confined. In fact, last night, he slapped me."

Gloria was more than aware that Barbara and her husband had a difficult marriage, and she had previously suggested that they seek marriage counseling. Barbara had taken her sister's advice, but was unable to continue the marriage counseling, because her husband refused to go to the sessions.

But this time, when Barbara told Gloria that her husband had actually hit her, Gloria said immediately, "Barbara, you need to get out of this relationship. Violence is inexcusable and you can never have a relationship that will work if you are beaten."

"But he's a good man," Barbara said. "And besides, what do you know? You've never even been married. You don't really know the pressure he's under at work. You don't know how hard it is for us to make ends meet."

Gloria then looked at Barbara and said, "Then why are you telling me about this in the first place? Why did you just start this conversation off saying that you wanted to leave him? Don't attack me. You need to take a good look at the relationship between you and your husband and how he is constantly attacking you."

What Barbara was doing was defending her man even though he beat her. Deep down inside she knew that this relationship was a terrible one. She was looking for a way to vent her anger and frustration by trying to start an argument with her sister.

Barbara is like so many people who can't face up to what their problem really is. They will try to use you as a scapegoat— try to initiate an argument—when there is really nothing to argue about.

Don't buy into it. If you see this type of behavior coming, just ward it off like Gloria did with Barbara. Refer to what the problem really is—in Barbara's case, her abusive husband—and don't allow yourself to be manipulated into an argument.

HOW TO DEAL WITH ARGUMENTATIVE PEOPLE

There are people who just love to pick a fight. These people are draining, and you need to get them out of your life. Some people actually like to be around argumentative people because they find them challenging and stimulating. Studies show, however, that most people don't like to be around people who are argumentative. These argumentative people try to elevate their own status by always being "right." If by chance you do encounter such a fight-picking person, be up front with them. Say, "You have contradicted everything I have said. Are you trying to pick a fight with me?" Oftentimes, it is not what the person says but how they say it that turns you off.

Sometimes a person's voice quality may be so whiny or offensive that even though they don't mean to sound bitchy or hostile, they actually do. If someone's tone of voice bothers you, let them know that it does, because you may not only be doing yourself a favor, you may be doing them a favor as well.

BICKERERS

We all know the stereotype of the little old lady who bickers or nitpicks about the slightest detail. If you make even the slightest error in saying something, the bickerer will be on your case immediately. It is as though they have a radar for detail. They're always looking for a fight.

Bickerers aren't always little old ladies. Bickerers cross every age group and socio-economic status. In fact, you may know couples who bicker among themselves and make you feel uncomfortable when you are around them. Listening to bickering couples can be annoying and aggravating. What it shows is a lack of respect for one another.

There is nothing uglier than having to go to dinner with a couple and listening to them bicker over the pettiest details of who said what to whom, or who did what—contradicting one another throughout the meal. One of my clients, Diane, was having a hard time putting up with the bickering between her friend Stephanie and her husband, Ted. They would invite her out to dinner and they would bicker with each other through the entire meal—about everything. For example, Ted was telling a story about some friends whose boat they went fishing on.

He said he caught some snapper. "It wasn't snapper," Stephanie snootily interjected. "It was grouper." "No, it was snapper," retorted Ted. "No," persisted Stephanie, "it was grouper. Remember, you said, 'I caught this big grouper!' " "Look Stephanie," he said, "I should know what I caught. I was there." "Hey, I was there, too," cried Stephanie. "And I know what a grouper looks like. And you caught a grouper!"

Finally, in order to stop them and to show her friends how ridiculous they were acting, she blurted out, "Now, children, let's have none of this bickering," and she saw looks of embarrassment cross their faces as they realized how immature they were acting.

If you find yourself caught between two bickerers, you need to set some limits. Honestly tell them that their constant bickering is making you feel very uncomfortable and that you don't like being around them.

You have to set your limits and have them accept and respect these limits, or limit your socializing with them.

BUTTON PUSHERS

The only way someone can push your buttons is if you let them, and if, of course, what they say rings true.

For instance, if someone calls you fat and you know you're not fat, they're not going to be pushing any of your buttons. But if you are fat and they call you fat, you'll get angry. Jill and Joanna were planning to go somewhere on their spring break from college, but all of the places Joanna suggested were beyond Jill's financial means. She just didn't come from a rich family like her friend did.

"What's the matter with you?" Joanna finally cried. "Can't you afford anything?" This really hurt Jill, who had always been self-conscious about the fact that she was from a poor family.

Joanna was not a habitual button pusher—she was just feeling frustrated at the time because she was having problems with her boyfriend. Without realizing it, she had taken her frustrations out on her friend, and she certainly knew what button to push.

If you are being victimized by a button-pushing friend—and

it is usually our friends who push our buttons because they are
the ones who know us well—you need to stop and let them
know immediately that their behavior is unacceptable. Say,
"You know, you are pushing my button, and you really hurt
my feelings." If they do it again, stop them again by saying,
"That's the second time you did that. I really don't appreciate
it. Are you really intent on hurting me?" If they continue, re-
consider the friendship.

DAMAGE CONTROL FOR ARGUMENTS

The best way to stop an argument is to recognize what you are
arguing about and what has been said, and then ask the question, HOW CAN WE MAKE THIS WORK?

If the person you are arguing with doesn't want to stop or
says, "We can't make it work because you are wrong," and just
goes on and on, stop them by using a deep, projected tone and
say, "LET'S STOP THIS NOW." Then be silent and refuse to
argue. Nobody can argue with themselves. It takes two to have
an argument.

Oftentimes, arguments can escalate so that a minor disagree-
ment can turn into a major battle. For example, two people
may have a difference of opinion, as was the case with a client
of mine and his girlfriend. My client, Robert, said that he
thought that it would be a better idea for their relationship if
they were to date other people. His girlfriend, on the other
hand, thought it was a terrible idea. "Look," she said, "How is
seeing other people going to help our relationship?"

"I think it will help our relationship a lot," he said, "because
it will give us a breather. We can see how we really feel about
each other." She said, "Well, you can take as long a breather
as you want, because I'm out of here. I don't ever want to see
you again."

My client tried to calm his girlfriend down, saying that he
wasn't ready to make a commitment and that they needed more
time, but his girlfriend wouldn't listen.

Whichever side you take in this story doesn't matter. What
matters is that the woman literally "threw the baby out with
the bathwater." She was angry, frustrated, and hurt. As a re-

sult, this argument—difference of opinion—resulted in the destruction of the relationship, whereas some very basic communication efforts on both of their parts could have saved the "baby" and the "bathwater."

ANGER AS A WEAPON IN ARGUING

When you are involved in an argument, most of the time you will get angry. However, there are things that you should never do, no matter how angry you get. You can yell, shout, scream, but never do any of the following if you want to maintain a lasting relationship.

1. NEVER NAME CALL. It can have a very devastating effect on someone. In private moments these names used in anger (i.e., "FAT PIG" or "UGLY SLOB" or "NASTY BITCH") are not easily forgotten. These names can resonate in a person's mind as they will now question whether these labels reflect their partner's true feelings about them.

2. NEVER HIT BELOW THE BELT. If your partner has told you something in confidence, such as a past incident they might not be proud of, bringing it up and throwing it back in their face is unconscionable. Doing this can diminish your partner's trust in you forever.

3. NEVER ACCUSE if you want results. Don't say "You never bring me flowers," or "You're always so lazy." Instead, bring up how you feel about their actions; i.e., "I feel neglected when I'm not remembered with flowers or a gift," or "It aggravates me so to see someone with such potential let laziness take over and not take advantage of who they are."

4. NEVER ARGUE JUST TO VENT ANGER. Make sure that your anger is directed at your mate's actions or behavior, not at someone else or something else in your life that's upsetting you.

5. DON'T SHUT YOUR MIND OFF and only think of your own point of view without being conscious and aware of what your partner is saying to you. Sometimes listening closely to what they said or the tone of their voice can give you a whole new insight into solving the issue at hand.

222 · LILLIAN GLASS, PH.D.

6. ALWAYS RECAP. Try to talk to your mate in terms of what you interpret their points of view to be and what yours are. Often in doing so you will discover that you both may share the same views after all, or that you have totally misinterpreted what your mate was trying to say. Each party recapping what the other's point of view is can only add to developing a closer bond between the couple.

USING TEARS AND HUMOR WHEN ARGUING

Even though laughter and tears may seem like the opposite ends of the continuum, they really are quite similar. They both often come out of frustration and are used to release anger toward another person.

Some people use tears because they feel victim-like when they are arguing. Sometimes people cry just because they can't express themselves any other way—especially verbally. Others deliberately use tears to manipulate or disarm their adversary and make them feel guilty or sorry for them. Whatever the motivation is, most people feel uncomfortable when there are tears during an argument, but if tears are your means of communication and it comes from the heart, go ahead and cry.

The same is true for humor. The only problem with humor is that some people will constantly use humor to avoid the argument—to avoid expressing their true feelings and to avoid facing the issues of the argument. This is very annoying and extremely frustrating if you are trying to get your point across. If someone is constantly making jokes of the issues you are trying to bring up, you need to stop them by saying, "Look, there's nothing funny about this. I'm serious, and I want to resolve this problem with you."

And yet, sometimes humor may be a good way of letting off some steam—allowing you to step back and make light and even laugh at yourself.

RESPECT—THE KEY TO REMEMBER WHEN ARGUING

No matter what your argument is about, no matter what the problem is, the one thing never to forget is your ultimate respect for the other person. I can't stress this enough.

If you love someone, you really never want to hurt them, but you do want to get your point across. One of my clients, a tennis professional, told me about a technique that her husband uses whenever they argue with one another that shows her how much he loves her. Whenever an argument gets out of hand, he will stop and hold her and say, "Honey, I don't want to argue with you. I love you. I want you to win. So let's not argue. Let's come to an agreement and work this out." This simple technique defuses the argument.

Instead of saying, "I love you," you may say, "Look, I really respect you. I don't want to argue with you. Let's just try to work this out." Whether it's a business or social relationship, the key is the word RESPECT—the respect you feel for the other person and your willingness to hear that person out, to listen to their point of view, and then try to come to a compromise.

You need to swallow your pride and literally put your ego in your back pocket and make a conscious effort to see the other person's point of view. Even if you don't agree with their point of view, it is important that you see where they are coming from. You may even learn something from them.

WINNING YOUR ARGUMENT

If you win an argument, be graceful about it. You don't want to gloat over your victory and say, "Hah! I told you so! You knew I was right!" You don't want to rub the other person's face in it. Simply say to the other person, "I'm really glad that you were able to see my point of view," and let the person feel comfortable about coming over to your point of view.

ADMITTING YOU'RE WRONG

It is just as important to know how to lose an argument as it is to know how to win one. When you do lose, don't throw up your arms and say in disgust, "Oh, alright, I guess I'm going to have to do it your way." Instead, be a lady or a gentleman about your defeat. Don't be a sore loser.

Admitting you are wrong is one of the biggest things a person can do. So many of my clients have said to me, "If only my father could have said, 'I'm sorry for what I did to you,' " or "If only my mother had said, 'I'm sorry for the way I treated you as a child,' " it would have made such a difference in their lives as adults and in the way they felt about their parents. It would have been such a warm, generous gesture on the part of their parents, if they only could have admitted they were wrong, but unfortunately, this rarely happens. It is a very special person who can do this.

If you are wrong, don't be afraid to admit it. Just say, "You're right, I was wrong, I can really see your point of view," or "I'm sorry, it was my misunderstanding," or "It was my mistake." It takes a person who has a lot of integrity and a healthy self-esteem to do this.

FORGIVING

According to the dictionary, the word *forgive* means to *give up*. It does not mean to forget, but simply to give up—to let things go. So when you have an argument with someone, forgiving them is simply letting go of the anger.

... 15 ...

Good Listening

One of the most important things you can learn from this book is how to listen to people. People have made mistakes, lost money, lost friends, and lost job opportunities and made poor business decisions just because they have been poor listeners.

Some of the Fortune 500 companies are so aware that listening skills can improve business—prevent mistakes and promote better employer-employee relationships—that they have employed communications specialists such as myself to teach their employees how to develop better listening skills. The military, the United States Senate, the Department of Labor, and the Army Office of Intelligence are only a few of the government agencies who have benefited from listening programs designed to help interpersonal relationships among employees. Listening programs have improved communications in critical job areas where crucial time had been taken away from more important work due to miscommunication.

Eighty percent of our waking day is spent communicating, and very few of us do it well because we are a society of such poor listeners. Listening is a lot more than just hearing. When you hear something, you are sensing a message. However, when you are listening, you are interpreting and analyzing what is said. Unfortunately, too many of us are so busy hearing what we want to hear that we are not listening to what is actually being said.

Almost every one of us finds a person who doesn't listen a complete turnoff. We are annoyed when people do not pay attention to us. In fact, a Gallup Poll I ran found that close to ninety percent of the people surveyed found the most annoying people to be those who interrupt and don't listen. It's frustrating to be around a person who doesn't listen because they negate your self-esteem.

Often we think we know what the other person is trying to say and we miss the point entirely. This happened to a client of mine, Linda. She wanted to purchase a very expensive watch to enhance her husband's image on the job after he had just been promoted. She found the watch at a discounted price. When she excitedly said to him, "Remember that Rolex watch you looked at in the window the other day?" Her husband, not even bothering to listen to the rest of what she was trying to say, cut her off and angrily blurted out, "I don't want to hear another word about it. You know we can't afford it. And that's that."

Had her husband bothered to listen to the rest of the story, he might have worn a new Rolex to his new job. Unfortunately, his wife returned the watch she had bought on sale the next day because she was so disgusted with her husband for not listening to what she had to say.

I might also add that Linda is not perfect, either. Instead of communicating with her husband and letting him know that his listening skills left a lot to be desired, she did not confront the problem, but instead returned the gift out of anger.

There are too many people who lose sight of what it is to have a good relationship with another person. They only way any relationship can work is to have good communication skills, including listening skills. "If only I had really listened, I would have realized that this relationship was ending," said a teary-eyed land developer whose girlfriend had just broken up with him.

My client was an extremely busy and controlling man who never really listened to anybody, including his girlfriend. Whenever she suggested something, he sloughed it off. He made all the plans, arrangements, and didn't let her have a say in anything. Disgusted with her status in the relationship, she told him that she needed him to listen to her, that she wanted to be a bigger part of his life. When she suggested that they go for counseling, his comment was, "You need it, not me. Why don't you go?" When she suggested that they go away for a vacation to spend some time alone together, he once again told her he was busy, and that now wasn't the right time.

Exasperated, she finally said one night at dinner, "I can't go on like this. I don't feel that you are respecting what I have to say. All you do is make jokes. You don't take me seriously. I feel like I'm just a showpiece for you." Once again, my client sloughed her off, saying, "Don't be so serious. Take it easy. Let's just have a good time and see how it works out." His girlfriend said, "Okay, but I'm only giving the relationship one more month, and if it doesn't work out, I'm moving out."

A month later her closets were empty. My client couldn't understand how she could do this to him. He couldn't understand why she would just leave him without warning.

I proceeded to refresh his memory about what his girlfriend had said to him a month earlier—that she would leave him, unless there was a change in his attitude toward her. He just didn't want to listen to what she was saying. Suddenly it was as though a light went on in his head as he realized that he would still have had a relationship with this woman if he had taken her more seriously and really "listened" to what she had to say.

People have difficulty listening to one another because they are so busy playing the *I think that you think that I think* game. We are so busy thinking about our own agendas and needs that we spend little time really listening to what the other person has to say.

Have you ever had a conversation with someone whom you felt wasn't even in the same room with you? Most people enter into conversation with a mind-set. They're not geared to hearing what the other person has to say.

A client of mine, a plastic surgeon, sees this all the time in his practice. People come into his office and they only hear what they want to hear. He could sit down and tell them one hundred times for one hour that he is certain that they will look better cosmetically than they do now, but he cannot guarantee that they will look like Catherine Deneuve or Robert Redford.

But many of his patients block what he is telling him. They don't listen when *he* tells them that the outcome of the surgery will depend on the way a person's skin heals, the shape and structure they presently have, and of course, the surgeon's skill. So many patients tend to be disappointed in the results, oftentimes because they haven't really *listened*.

LISTENING TO A PERSON'S BODY LANGUAGE

You can read a lot about a person by the way they come across physically—by the way they move, by their posture, their gestures, their facial expressions. In observing a person's body language, you are literally "listening" to their body talk.

I recently saw a newspaper article that had a picture of one of my clients, a well-known politician. In the photograph, he looked tense. He was hunched over, he looked angry, brooding. Knowing him as well as I did, I called him and told him that I had seen his picture in the newspaper and that he looked troubled.

"You're right," he said. "I was unhappy," and then he proceeded to tell me why.

"Visual listening" can make an enormous difference in your ability to detect people's moods and to achieve more honest, open communication.

This involves looking at the following areas: facial expression, body language, gestures, and vocal patterns. We've all read enough books, such as Jules Fast's and David Givens's books on body language, which talk about how you can read another person by the way they look and move. It's also obvious from spending time with a person that you can detect certain moods that may be based on their facial expression. My previous book, *Talk to Win*, provides information on how you can detect a person's feelings, mood, and even personality by listening to how they express themselves through their various vocal patterns.

The key to good listening is to pay attention and to be aware of all body, facial, and vocal patterns.

FAKING ATTENTION

Some people may appear to be a good listeners, but their minds are elsewhere. I would much rather talk to a person who is really listening to me, but who happens to be doing other things, than to a person who is giving me all of their *non-attention*.

Some people are multi-processors, which means that they can do a number of things at once—i.e., talk on the phone, write a memo, and listen to your story. You might not think that these people are very focused, but you would be surprised at how very focused they actually are. These people often don't feel comfortable unless they are doing a lot of things at once.

On the other hand, there are people who are "compartmentalized" processors, who can only focus their attention on one thing at a time. These people feel comfortable only when they are doing one thing, and then they go on to the next thing.

Neither type is right or wrong in the way they listen. Just be aware that people process information in either one of these two ways.

Whether a person is a multi-processor of a compartmentalized processor, they can still fake listening. Most of us have experienced the person who nods understandingly throughout a conversation and in reality doesn't hear a thing we are saying to them. Therefore, it is essential for you to constantly "check in." Use phrases like: "Does this make sense to you? . . . Do you understand what I am saying? . . . What are your feelings about what I just said? . . . Can you explain to me in your own terms what I have just said to you?"

If they can answer these questions intelligently, then you can rest assured that they have actually been listening to you.

INTERRUPTING

What do you say to the person who constantly interrupts you and breaks your train of thought? You need to be *direct*. Stop the conversation *immediately* and say, "Please stop interrupting me," or "Let me finish first." You need to use these short, abrupt phrases, and then pause for a few seconds, in silence. Sometimes people will be so rude that they will not even hear you telling them not to interrupt you. In this case, take a breath in, hold it, bear down on your stomach muscles, and bellow out in a loud voice, "PLEASE LET ME FINISH WHAT I WAS SAYING." Perhaps the best response I've heard to someone who kept interrupting them was, "Would you *please* give me *two* minutes out of the *sixty* minutes you took to make a point?" If this still doesn't work, you may want to place your hand firmly on their arm, look directly into their eyes, and once again repeat: "Please let me finish what I was saying." If that doesn't work, and your impulse is to punch them, leave immediately! Just walk away. They'll get the message.

Now obviously this is an extreme situation. Most people aren't that rude. Usually, if you make an interrupter aware of their bad habit on a consistent basis, they'll usually get the message and try to control themselves.

If you know that you have a problem of interrupting people, one of the ways you can break this bad habit is through the breathing technique that I have mentioned throughout this book. Before you are ready to jump in—suck some air in, hold it for a few seconds, and as you are holding it, really listen to what the other person is saying.

LISTENING AND STILL NOT GETTING THE POINT

Have you ever spent time with someone who thought you were paying attention to what they were saying and then suddenly realized that you had no idea what they were talking about at all? What most likely happened was that they changed the subject. If you have problems following a conversation, you need to stop the speaker and say, "Hold on a minute, I'm not following what you just said," or "Weren't we just talking about something else?" or "Excuse me, I'm lost."

Using these key phrases will usually get them back on track. A good listener will not be afraid to interject and let the speaker know that they weren't comprehending what was being said.

If you, on the other hand, want to change the subject midstream, you need to let your listener know what you are doing so they can follow your train of thought. Some key phrases for interrupting yourself are: "By the way," or "To change the subject for a moment," or "This is a sidebar," or "I'll get back to what I'm saying, but I just want to digress for a moment."

STOP BEING JUDGMENTAL

If you're too judgmental a person, you're not going to be a good listener, because you have most likely already formulated your opinion before the other person has finished saying what they have to say. Your judgment, in a sense, forms a wall—a barrier—which makes it difficult for information to get through to you.

It's human nature that we all make judgments. We all have our prejudices—right or wrong—but if we are to be good listeners, we need to drop all of these prejudices. We need to stop judging and start listening.

It's difficult to create a blank slate in your mind and allow people to be themselves and not judge them—to actually hear what they say and process what they are saying, not what you think they are saying. One of my friends, George, has an uncanny ability to attract people to him. He is so open and warm, and people tend to gravitate toward him. After watching him at a party I realized why people like him so much. It's because he openly accepts people. He doesn't judge them or evaluate them. He just accepts them for what they are.

For most of us, being like George takes a lot of practice. I encourage my clients to actually practice meeting people, and forcing themselves, as difficult as it may seem, not to judge people but to listen to what they have to say.

If you catch yourself being judgmental, you may want to try picturing a blackboard with all of your prejudices written on it in chalk and then mentally visualize yourself taking an eraser and wiping it clean.

YOUR SPEAKING ABILITY CAN
IMPEDE THE LISTENER

Many communication researchers have pleaded for the listener to judge the content of what a person is saying and not the delivery. I tend to disagree with this completely.

If a person has a poor delivery, it can tell you a lot about the kind of person they are. Oftentimes, how a person sounds reflects their personality or psychological state. According to UCLA researcher and linguist Dr. Christine Baltaxe, a person's psychological state can be determined by the sound of their voice. Even though a person may present a vocal pattern that does not accurately represent who they are, people still react to them as if they had these traits. For example, if a person is very successful in business but has a very boring, monotonous voice that dies off at the end, the listener will react to the person they "hear" rather than to the person they actually are.

It may not seem fair, but research shows that people *do* judge you, respect you, or disrespect you based on the way you speak. If you have a loud, obnoxious tone, a high-pitched baby-like voice, a piercing, nasal whine, a graveling, grating voice, a lisp or a stuttering problem, there is no question that people will and *do* perceive you more negatively than if you had a pleasant speaking voice.

One of the most difficult things for anyone to do is to listen to an irritating speaker, because the message almost always gets lost. If you do have a poor speaking voice, chances are that people's judgments of how you sound will get in the way of their hearing what you have to say. If you need help, you can follow the simple steps outlined in *Talk to Win*. Or seek professional help.

TIPS FOR BEING A GOOD LISTENER

There have been many researchers, such as Dr. Lyman Steele at the University of Minnesota, who have done a great deal of work in the area of listening. Dr. Steele states that there are primarily four basic stages in the listening process. They are:

1. Sensing information, which is where you receive the information in an auditory fashion;
2. Interpreting the information, where you are, in essence, putting it in your mental computer and processing it;
3. Evaluating the information, where you see how what

has been said relates to you, or how it fits into your own way of thinking;

4. Responding to what was said to you emotionally, intellectually, and physically.

Here are some tips that can help improve your listening skills, which can in turn improve your relationships personally and professionally.

1. *Develop an active listening posture:* Lean forward, maintain good eye contact, nod to insure that the other person knows you understand what is being said.

2. *Eliminate annoying habits:* Biting your lower lip while you are listening to someone, tapping a pencil, clicking your finger, or playing with an object while you are listening can be very disconcerting.

3. *Pay attention to ideas, not facts:* If someone makes an incorrect statement of fact, don't focus entirely on the small blunder, but listen instead to the ideas being communicated, even though you may be so detail oriented that you miss the overall point. Look at the forest, not the trees.

4. *Keep your emotions in check:* Even though it is good to be able to respond to someone emotionally, don't focus on emotionally laden words and lose sight of everything else that was said. For example, if someone calls women "gals," even if you hate the term, try to hear *all* of what the person has to say. Even though this word may offend you personally, you need to keep your emotions in check in order to process the complete message. Then you can react accordingly.

5. *Ask questions:* Don't be afraid to ask questions or to ask the person to elaborate further, in order to gather more data. This can also stimulate further conversation.

6. *Don't jump to conclusions:* No one likes to have a sentence finished for them. Not only is this disrespectful, but the conclusion jumper is often wrong.

7. *Try to stay focused:* Even though it is difficult to focus or concentrate on something one hundred percent of the time, make it a point to become *unpreoccupied* when you are listening to someone. Don't think about the fight you just had

with your boss, the date you're going to have that evening, or how much time you have left on the parking meter. You owe it to the other person to give them your complete, undivided attention. This requires a lot of practice. If you catch yourself wandering, go back to establishing eye contact and "facial" contact, because this will oftentimes re-focus you.

Being a good listener is essential to being a good communicator. It's a two-way street that involves listening and reacting to what has been said. It's a continuous, flowing process, like a good game of tennis, where you serve and return. It's a give-and-take experience where there is an action and a reaction. The continuous give-and-take of the volley into each other's court is what makes a meaningful, interactive conversation possible.

Dr. Lillian Glass is recognized as one of the world's foremost authorities on communication skills and self-image. A speech pathologist in private practice in Beverly Hills, she has coached scores of celebrities, sports figures, politicians, and corporate executives, as well as the general public. The author of *How to Deprogram Your Valley Girl, Talk to Win,* and *World of Words,* Dr. Glass has appeared nationally on such programs as *Oprah Winfrey, Today, CBS Evening News,* and *Sonya Live* and has been featured in *The New York Times, The Washington Post, People,* and *USA Today.*

WHERE TO GET MORE INFORMATION

If you wish to receive more personalized information, please send this page in a SELF-ADDRESSED, STAMPED envelope to:

Dr. Lillian Glass
c/o Your Total Image, Inc.
435 N. Bedford Drive, Suite 209
Beverly Hills, Calif. 90210

or call (213) 274-0528

Name_____

Address_____

City, State, Zip Code_____

Phone number (   )_____

            area code

Please send me information on the following:

_____ Additional Books by Dr. Glass
_____ Audiotapes
_____ Videotapes
_____ Lectures to Companies
_____ Group Seminars in your City
_____ Workshops
_____ Private Sessions
_____ Telephone Evaluations with Dr. Glass
_____ Personal Evaluations with Dr. Glass
_____ Accent Reduction or Instruction
_____ Aquiring an Accent or Dialect
_____ Stuttering Therapy
_____ Speech and Language Therapy
_____ Voice Improvement
_____ Communication Skill Improvement
_____ Audiotape Evaluation of Your Voice
_____ Newsletter

Index